FROM THE MAKERS OF T...

COUNT ME IN

THE DARING LIFE *of a* JESUS FOLLOWER

Travis Agnew with
Alex Kendrick & Stephen Kendrick

PUBLISHING®
BRENTWOOD, TENNESSEE

CONTENTS

DARING DISCIPLESHIP

Don't settle for following Jesus halfway.

IT'S CHALLENGING TO BE A teenager these days. Many students comment on the stress during these pivotal years, brought on by peer pressure, unending homework assignments, relational dramas, tempting situations, and demanding authority figures. Although this time of life has always been full of unique challenges for every generation, no doubt yours is experiencing an increasing amount of adversity. If you feel overwhelmed, we get it.

Being your age *is* challenging. But we want to offer a different type of challenge: in your journey from childhood to adulthood, what if you could thrive in the opportunity instead of just survive through the opposition? We hope and pray you live these years as a dedicated follower of Jesus, eagerly seeking His ways and diligently maturing in crucial areas. Don't waste these years; use them intentionally. If you do, you will grow by leaps and bounds spiritually and set the trajectory of your life on following Jesus intently.

Restraint Versus Responsibility

One of the most consistent hardships you feel during these years is probably the awkward tension between restraint and responsibility. As you age, you will become more convinced you can handle situations independently. You don't think you need as many rules from your parents. You might inwardly think or verbally process that you know better than many authority figures in your life. Other people might bothersomely not agree that you are as capable as you feel.

In one sense, you might feel frustrated that some people still treat you like a child. In another sense, you don't want all the responsibilities of an adult, because some of those don't seem that fun. Some people annoy you by explaining too much, while others overwhelm you by expecting too much. The tension between restraint and responsibility can be exhausting.

Maybe you want more freedom when it comes to driving but less responsibility when it comes to cleaning. You want the ability to spend what you want but not be forced to work when you would rather not. The years between graduating elementary school and graduating high school are full of unbalanced expectations. At the heart of it, you probably feel frustrated when someone treats you like a child, because you should be respected as being closer to an adult than that. You want more responsibility, but you also want people to affirm your potential and to respect you.

Many people demand a lot from students but don't expect much. That's not the same with Jesus. If you've ever wanted someone to treat you with high expectations and provide you with exciting privileges, you've come to the right place. Jesus isn't waiting for you to get a job to develop a purpose. He's not waiting for you to move out on your own before He asks you to step out in faith. Do you want to be respected for what you can do at your age? Then get ready.

Reimagining the Teen Years

When Justin started following Jesus as a teenager, he went all in. He remembers the day of his baptism with sincere joy. He wasn't sure what was supposed to happen next, but he was eager to find out. Some mentors at his church helped him start his first Bible reading plan, connected him with other guys his age who wanted to grow, and answered his growing set of questions. Justin was most surprised, though, when his church gave him opportunities to serve. He thought that was just for adults who had gone to Bible college. But the church let him teach alongside a mentor, and he improved weekly.

Raising the bar in the church caused Justin to step up in his commitment to Jesus. He didn't try to hide his faith at school. He started being intentional with other teens who lived near him, always bringing a few of them along to church. He grew so quickly, and it was all because people around him expected him to do more than the bare minimum. Suppose Justin had waited until he was an adult before serving Christ seriously. Can you imagine how many people would have missed his example and impact?

Jesus doesn't limit your potential because of your youthfulness. If you are ready to follow Him now, He won't keep you in a waiting room until later. Your current "teen" label is a human invention, anyway, and a fairly recent one at that. Did you know that the word *teenager* wasn't in the dictionary until the 1940s? It wasn't a word because it wasn't needed. No "in-between" stage of life kept young people from becoming responsible adults, and growing maturity was expected from young people as soon as they left childhood behind.

Companies in the 1940s originated the word *teenager* to make money off that generation.[1] After the Great Depression, these companies saw a great opportunity to make money by targeting these newly coined *teenagers* with "must-have" products. The term became popular and began to represent people ages thirteen to eighteen who now wanted the same stuff as their peers to fit in.

Unlike these original teenagers, you don't have to settle for years of mediocrity between childhood and adulthood. Why wait to do something great when God has used people your age many times before?

- Joseph was seventeen years old when God began showing him future events for which he needed to prepare (Genesis 37:2).
- Miriam was not even old enough for the youth group when she diligently watched over her baby brother Moses and created a brilliant plan while talking to a member of the intimidating royal family (Exodus 2:4–7).
- Samuel was a boy when God called him into service (1 Samuel 3:8).
- David's father might have thought his son's young age kept him from being considered for something important, but God thought David was just right for the job (1 Samuel 16:7, 11).
- When God enlisted the prophet Jeremiah to preach to God's people at one of the most pivotal times in history, Jeremiah was still a youth (Jeremiah 1:6).

Those are only a few of the young people God used through-out Scripture. There are more! For thousands of years, young men and women around the world have continued to passion-ately pursue Christ. God doesn't want you to wait to be passion-ate about Him and His cause. You might grow up inactive and believe that's the norm, but that would be a shame! Even if your peers or authority figures remain spiritually lazy, that doesn't have to be your standard. Jesus is too great and glorious to follow Him halfway.

Youthful Example

The apostle Paul believed a young man named Timothy was far more capable than most people would have given someone his age credit for. Paul watched Timothy transform from a young boy learning from his godly mother and grandmother into a bold pastor with reliable character (2 Timothy 1:5; 4:2).

Part of Timothy's growth was due to Paul's influence. Timothy was both a disciple of Jesus and a disciple of Paul. Jesus had ascended to heaven before Timothy ever got to meet Him, but Timothy knew Him very well. How? Because Paul told his young disciple what Jesus was like. Paul and Timothy were so close that Paul called him his "true son in the faith" (1 Timothy 1:2). It was one mentor giving everything he had to one follower. They called it discipleship.

This is the context for one of the most repeated Bible verses in youth groups worldwide. As Timothy stepped into ministry leadership, Paul wrote to him, "Don't let anyone despise your youth, but set an example for the believers in speech, in conduct, in love, in faith, and in purity" (1 Timothy

4:12). It was Paul's loving yet bold warning to his young disciple: don't let your age be an excuse for slacking off.

Paul knew Jesus could use Timothy, even if others didn't think he was old enough yet. Timothy wasn't the backup option because the starter injured himself. Paul wouldn't let Timothy waste pivotal years of youthful energy combined with maturing discipleship. The time was too valuable and the possibility too remarkable. Timothy wasn't the church of the future; he was the church of the present, and Paul was ready for Timothy to be a leader within it.

Like Timothy, you can be an example to all people, regardless of their age. Paul told Timothy exactly how to affect those who observed his life: let the content of your words (speech) and the character of your life (conduct) be done with the right motive (love), with the right focus (faith), and in the right way (purity). Paul's call to Timothy is the same one God is giving you through His Word. Don't misuse these years on lesser pursuits. Avoid responding to God with a list of excuses for why you can't do anything now. The Almighty God can work mightily through willing young people, including you.

If you feel willing but unprepared, you might be missing a critical component: discipleship. Before Jesus ascended into heaven, He commanded His followers to go and make disciples (Matthew 28:19). The term *disciple* means "student." A disciple is someone who desires to learn a certain way of living from a trustworthy example. Jesus calls His followers to teach others "to observe everything I have commanded you" (Matthew 28:20).

Maybe you are saved, but has someone discipled you? Jesus called us to make disciples, not converts. Following

Jesus is more than saying a prayer, raising a hand, getting baptized, or kneeling at an altar. Your baptism is an important step, but it shouldn't be the last one. You were baptized publicly to announce to people in the room, "The work is now beginning; keep me accountable," not "The job is done; leave me alone."

Discipleship requires more than a momentary commitment with no follow-through. We've all had moments of sincere motivation to make changes. Maybe you felt the pull to continue your positive trends as camp wrapped up last summer. You might have heard a sermon that convicted you to make a lasting change. Or maybe someone else's example encouraged you to be and do more.

You felt those urges. You knew there were things you should start doing. You were convinced there were some things you should stop doing.

But it's one thing to say you want to follow Jesus and another to do it. Responding to the gospel happens in a moment. Following Jesus as His disciple, though, will continue throughout your life. Discipleship means admitting you have been changed by grace but still desire change by growth. Embracing discipleship is the honest acknowledgment that you have room to grow and eagerly desire to do so.

Peter is Jesus's most famous disciple. He is well known for his amazing accomplishments and his embarrassing failures. After three years of following Jesus, Peter had a moment to prove himself. Jesus had been arrested, and a young girl identified Peter as one of Jesus's disciples. Instead of boldly stepping forward in faith, he denied Jesus in fear. Peter should have been standing beside Jesus, but he was warming himself beside a fire (John 18:18), more focused on his comfort than Christ.

The next time we see Peter standing near a fire, he wasn't running from Jesus. He was running toward Him (John 21:7). Jesus rose from the grave and still sought out the disciples who had abandoned Him. He called to them while they were in a boat fishing. Peter didn't try to walk on water this time; he plunged into the sea and swam the rest of the way. As he approached the shore, he saw Jesus, who was cooking break-fast over a fire. The scene had to be eerily familiar. It likely jogged Peter's memory. As he stared at a reminder of when he gave into fear, situated next to the Savior he had failed, Peter probably was at a loss for what to say.

Maybe you feel you have failed Jesus when it counted the most too. Let this scene by the fire remind you that Jesus hasn't given up on you. He is willing to move past moments of letdowns and provide second chances. Jesus calls each of us to discipleship—not perfection. Even if your past is full of missed opportunities, there's a Savior on the shore inviting you to sit by Him at the fire and give following Him another shot.

No matter what has happened in the past, what will you do now? Many students say they follow Jesus, but only the ones who keep moving toward Him are serious about their com-mitment. We invite you to sign up for the most life-changing experience and Jesus's world-changing plan. Will you say "yes" to Jesus's daring life of true discipleship?

How to Read This Book

Where will you begin? We want you to look at the life of the master disciple-maker Himself, Jesus. In this book, we will highlight eight priorities Jesus gave His disciples. You will also see these priorities for yourself by reading the Gospel of Luke, which gives an account of Jesus's life and His discipleship of others. Luke has twenty-four chapters, so you will read three chapters in Luke's Gospel for each chapter in *Count Me In*. We will guide your reading and show you what to look for as you go through each section of Scripture.

If you read this book on your own, we applaud that you're prioritizing discipleship. Your best chance to succeed at being one of Jesus's disciples, though, is by having people in your life who are at least aware of your process, if not joining you in it. Do you have a discipleship mentor (parent, pastor, coach, teacher) or a friend? You could read this book with a group or another person, or you could share what you are learning with your mentor or someone you are discipling.

Some people your age will hear this call and think they are too young. They might say, "Count me out," because they don't think they're ready. Another's response could sound like, "Count me in later," because they have more pressing pursuits. But don't you want something more? If Jesus is this captivating (and He is!), why would you wait to follow Him?

Will you say, "Count me in!" to a daring life as a Jesus follower? If so, take the next step in your discipleship by joining us in reading the Gospel of Luke and working through this book. ·*ˆ

1. https://dp.la/exhibitions/children-progressive-era/childhood-postwar-america/teenage-culture#

~~~ 2 ~~~

DILIGENT DEVOTIONS

You can't follow Jesus unless you use the
Bible to know where He's going.

IF YOU DARE TO FOLLOW Jesus where He leads, you must clarify something immediately: the direction He's going. How can you determine that? You find His will, or His direction, in the Bible, the Word of God.

Within the pages of the Bible, you learn to love what God loves. You better understand how to value what He prioritizes. If you attempt to live for God without consulting His Word, you will fall victim to a temptation that goes back to Adam and Eve. They doubted God's love and good plans for them, and that doubt made them vulnerable to Satan's deceitful words. Just like Adam and Eve, once you doubt God's Word, you will be tempted and might even start to make up your own rules for what is right and what is wrong.

We need the Bible. Jesus uses it to communicate everything we need to follow Him on the path of discipleship. We know, we know . . . the Bible is a really long book. You already have a lot of textbooks crammed in your backpack and documents stuffed in your folders. Even if you like to read, the Bible is a complex book, full of sayings that don't always translate easily into our text-chat-emoji-filled world.

Plus, if you were intrigued by this daring call to a radical lifestyle, you might think the idea just got watered down by encouraging you to read an ancient book. But if that's the case, you're thinking of Scripture in the wrong way. If you believe the Bible is nothing but a dull book archiving a rigid belief system, then it's no surprise you're not eager to read it. But here's the reality: Scripture is the opposite of boring.

Scripturally Unmotivated

Beth's small group leader gave a challenge that seemed difficult at first: read one chapter from 1 Peter each day for five days. Beth had never read the Bible consistently. She reluctantly told her leader she would try to do what she asked.

Once Beth got home, she realized she couldn't read one chapter a day. She read two. She was so mesmerized by what she read in the first chapter that she kept going. By the time her small group gathered the following Sunday, she had studied 1 Peter numerous times and was amazed at all the truths about Jesus she had learned. She began to see the Bible wasn't a boring book at all. She finally understood how important the Scriptures were to her. All it took was an intentional disciple-maker (her small group leader) and a clear goal (read one chapter from 1 Peter each day for five days).

Imagine all the students in your school are struggling with a disease. Unless something changes, they will die by the end of the year. Many people attempt to help them, but the more solutions they try, the worse the students' symptoms become. In their fear, they turn on each other rather than go to each other for support. Their condition worsens by the day.

Then, amazingly, you discover a cure. You don't develop it yourself; you receive specific instructions for curing the sick and wiping out what is endangering them. The instructions come from an expert who has successfully healed countless others with the same disease. He has graciously written down His notes and delivered them to you.

Would such a book be boring? Of course not! You would read it diligently, with unwavering focus, thinking of all your friends who need to be healed. No way would you let its difficult parts slow you down from getting to the cure. If research helps you understand unfamiliar words better, it doesn't seem like a chore. And you definitely don't feel the need to take a break and scroll through your phone. Nothing can sidetrack you when you know the cure is so readily available.

That imagined scenario helps you understand the power of Scripture. A compassionate and gracious God created all of us in His image, but we have tried to remodel ourselves after the templates of this world. We turn from what gives life to that which poisons our souls. All of us are sinners, and there's no hope of healing ourselves on our own. Our sin put us to death.

But God sent His Son, Jesus, to infect Himself with our sins. Jesus never did anything wrong, yet He identified with our weaknesses so that we could be made clean. Jesus's death provided the antidote each of us needs for our soul sickness. We call it the gospel, and it is truly good news.

Not only does the Bible provide that cure, but it also provides direction for so many of life's challenging situations. It gives clear guidance for anyone who feels isolated, fearful, anxious, depressed, or hopeless.

Did you know the Bible teaches how to leverage your life to make it count for more than just getting through it? Do you know that it speaks of an unseen war all around us in which God will be the ultimate victor? God invites us to join Him on the frontlines, rescuing countless lives from humanity's great enemy.

If we think the Bible is uninteresting, our boredom speaks more to what we're doing *with* its words than what is *in* them. The first step in discipleship is committing to learning about God's Word and how every phrase points us to the Savior.

Jesus and the Scriptures

As we follow Jesus on the path of discipleship, we discover the Word was central to His life on earth. *Count Me In* is designed to rally you to study the Bible more consistently than ever before, because it is the most important book. It holds the cure for our souls.

After reading this chapter, you will study how Jesus prioritized discipleship in Luke 1–3. Before you begin reading in Luke, we want you to be on the lookout for some key aspects. In those chapters Jesus not only says Scripture is necessary, but His example of relying on Scripture also convinces you of this truth even more.

Written Account

The book of Luke is not an autobiography where some ancient religious man wrote what he thought about himself. Not in the least. Luke, an educated doctor, wrote the book as a biography about Jesus. Luke identified key events, interviewed numerous sources, and investigated outrageous claims. The more Luke uncovered, the greater his faith grew. He was so sure of what he discovered that he wrote it down and shared it with his friend Theophilus (Luke 1:1-3).

Luke wrote the book for us too. He wanted his findings to prompt our investigation "so that you may know the certainty of the things about which you have been instructed" (Luke 1:4). His diligence paid off. His account still exists today, and it has been translated into hundreds of languages worldwide.

Luke felt the need to write his account down, and so did other biblical authors. It is so important to have God's instructions written down, for without that, everyone would decide on their own what was right or wrong. Without God revealing truth to us, we would be tempted to either exaggerate or downplay what we ought to do.

Kept Promises

Luke collected more information than the other gospel authors (Matthew, Mark, and John) about the events leading up to Jesus's birth. It seems that Luke interviewed Jesus's mother, Mary, and even Jesus's uncle, Zechariah, who encountered an angel and experienced a miraculous event.

Zechariah understood God's plan was happening right before his eyes, and he sang, "Just as he spoke by the mouth of his holy prophets in ancient times" (Luke 1:70). What do these words mean? They point to the power of Scripture. Zechariah had studied what we know as the Old Testament. He knew God's promises about the coming Messiah, and he was watching them miraculously be fulfilled right before his eyes. God "remembered his holy covenant" (Luke 1:72). Zechariah was amazed at how God kept His promises.

Scripture reminds us that God always keeps His promises, which helps us believe that God will continue to do so. That trait is often lacking in human relationships. How often have you been let down by people who failed to keep their word? That hurt is real. But although people may disappoint us, God always delivers on what He says He will do. The more you read the Bible, the more you will trust the only One who never breaks His promises.

Obeyed Instructions

Jesus's parents obeyed God's instructions. They set God above their desires or other people's expectations. As new parents attempting to figure out married life and parenthood, they knew one clear, yet pivotal strategy: (1) study the Scriptures, (2) obey the Scriptures, and (3) repeat steps 1 and 2.

Mary and Joseph read and obeyed what God told them to do. They did "just as it is written in the law of the Lord" (Luke 2:23). One of their first visits as a family of three was to the temple because it was "customary under the law" (Luke 2:27). In fact, they didn't get comfortable in their own home until after "they had completed everything according to the law of the Lord" (Luke 2:39). Such a commitment to Scripture started Jesus's family out with the right direction and determination.

Obedience is more important than we can imagine. Applying God's Word to our lives not only shows we're trying to be faithful to Him but also provides insights into how we can better flourish in this life. Scripture would feel disconnected from our lives if it were only a book about what other people attempted for God. But it's not. It's not just a book about what others did, but an invitation into what you can do. You can join

God in changing this world. How? By remembering His Word does not just provide information to consider. It gives you a purpose to fulfill and commands to obey.

Eager Student

If the events surrounding a baby's birth or the example of young parents don't connect with you, what about a scene from Jesus's life when He was around middle school age?

When Jesus was twelve, He participated in a Bible study. Not only did He attend it, but He also refused to leave it. Jesus, His parents, and His extended family all traveled to the temple in Jerusalem to celebrate a festival. But when His family began the journey home, Jesus wasn't with them. Maybe Mary thought Joseph had seen Jesus or vice versa, but regardless, He was missing.

Jesus might have been missing from the travel party, but He was exactly where He wanted to be. "After three days, they [Mary and Joseph] found him in the temple sitting among the teachers, listening to them and asking them questions. And all those who heard him were astounded at his understanding and his answers" (Luke 2:46–47). Think about it. How many middle-schoolers do you know who would choose to hang out with older religious teachers for a three-day Bible study?

Jesus wasn't your typical youth, and He doesn't want you to settle for that either. At twelve, He eagerly studied the Word, and He intentionally listened to older teachers. Some students find it challenging to answer questions in a Bible study, but Jesus was asking the teachers questions. He took advantage of an opportunity to gather with students of the Word and hear their thoughts. Those who listened to Him were amazed at His focused attention and thoughtful insights.

Showing Up

At the end of this event, Luke wrote this eye-opening description: "And Jesus increased in wisdom and stature, and in favor with God and with people" (Luke 2:52). Jesus experienced more than physical growth. He grew in wisdom and favor too.

You've probably met older people who remark on how much you've grown since the last time they saw you. If it's been a while or if you've recently experienced a growth spurt, they may be relentless in telling you that you are growing—as if you are somehow unaware.

But what if people saw growth in you that couldn't be recorded on a doctor's chart? Imagine growing in wisdom so much that others notice. Think about how they would respond if your understanding of the truth led to applying that truth to your life. You would change, and your changes would be so significant that others couldn't help but notice. Your commitment to following God would bring glory to God and good to others.

That type of growth doesn't happen by accident. What can you do about your physical height? I wouldn't think anything. But you can do a lot about how you develop wisdom. Where can you find it? In the Bible. "For the LORD gives wisdom; from his mouth come knowledge and understanding" (Proverbs 2:6).

Jesus taught we must depend upon Scripture because its words come from the very mouth of God (Matthew 4:4). That's why you can't grow apart from the Bible. You can try, and you might have limited success. But you won't grow anything long-lasting.

We get into danger when we receive hints of truth from others without learning how to get truth directly from God's Word. If you haven't been a regular student of God's Word but experienced some spiritual growth, it is because someone was teaching you Scripture. The power wasn't in the setting, situation, or speaker; it was in Scripture.

If you've wondered why you're not growing as a disciple of Jesus, that's the reason: you haven't yet committed to regularly eating from God's Word. Maybe you read someone's devotional. Perhaps you watched a video from a Christian influencer. But if you don't commit to coming to the table yourself, you are simply snacking while a feast is available. If your Bible intake is reading a single verse here or seeing a social media post there, it's like taking a breath mint. It will freshen you up for the next interaction, but it cannot and will not satisfy your hunger for the long haul. That's why, when Jesus was in the wilderness for forty days—hungry, lonely, thirsty, and tired—and the devil tempted Him, Jesus quoted Scripture: "Man must not live on bread alone but on every word that comes from the mouth of God" (Matthew 4:4; Deuteronomy 8:3). Follow Jesus's example. Don't settle for a mint when you need a meal.

Or think of it this way. If you wouldn't travel in the dark without a light, why would you attempt to navigate this world without God's Word, which is a lamp to your feet and a light to your path (Psalm 119:105)? No serious warrior would enter the battlefield without a weapon in hand, so you shouldn't navigate your life without the Word of God as your steady offense (Hebrews 4:12; Ephesians 6:17). In a world where trends pass quickly, why wouldn't you ground yourself in God's Word, which never passes away (Matthew 24:35; Isaiah 40:8)?

Count Me In for Diligent Devotions

If you are ready to say "yes" to Jesus's call for discipleship, you cannot do it apart from God's Word. Feeling guilty won't sustain you. A sense of obligation won't last long. You must see this commitment to reading, studying, and applying God's Word as essential for the growth you hope to experience.

Where do you start? Not necessarily at the beginning. The Bible is made up of sixty-six books. The Old Testament contains thirty-nine of them, while the New Testament has twenty-seven. These books range in size and differ in style. All Scripture is given by God, but not all its parts are as easily understandable as others. At least, not at first.

Many people commit to reading the Bible in large chunks without first getting consistent with smaller reps. But think about it: no one goes from passively watching sports from the stands to actively competing on the field. Training is involved. It takes time. As you develop muscles, you can handle more challenges and find gradual success.

That's why we want you to start with the Gospel of Luke. At the end of this study, you will have read an incredible account of Jesus and completed one book of the Bible, with only sixty-five to go! Discipleship is all about progress. As your consistency in reading Scripture grows, you will be amazed to discover that what once seemed difficult becomes much easier for you.

To build consistent devotion to Scripture, we recommend a few items:

1. **PLAN.** We have selected your Bible reading plan for these next few weeks, but you need to commit to another one after completing this book. With each plan, get intentional. Know the details before you start. How much time do you need to set aside? What time of day will you do it? How can you remove distractions and stay focused?

2. **PARTNER.** Share your plan with at least one other person for accountability. Maybe you have a friend doing this study with you—that will be a great help! Or perhaps you have a parent, pastor, or mentor who is intentional about your spiritual growth. Inform that person of your plan and invite them to ask you how it is going.

3. **PONDER.** Consider what needs to be memorized or applied. We've left space for you to jot down insights as you read. Note what sticks out to you. What did you learn about Jesus? How should you respond to what you observed?

4. **PERSIST.** Don't give up when you mess up. Bible reading is one of the only commitments where people often quit altogether if they miss reading a couple of times. But if you skip lunch today, you won't give up on dinner, will you? No, you'll find a drive-thru and get some food in your stomach as soon as possible because you are starving. Stay hungry for the Word! If you miss a day or a season, open the Bible back up once you come to your senses and get going again.

Are you ready to begin? Your path of discipleship starts with your commitment to God's Word. The Bible is a blessing to apply, not a burden to avoid. Can we count you in for diligent devotions?

Insights

1. What distracts you the most from reading God's Word?

   _____

   _____

   _____

   _____

2. List three steps you might take to lessen the pull of that distraction.

   _____

   _____

   _____

   _____

   _____

3. Who can you partner with to read the Bible?

   _____

   _____

   _____

   _____

4. Who is someone you believe knows the Bible well?

_____

_____

_____

_____

_____

5. Ask that person to tell you about a practice he or she uses to study the Bible, and try to implement that practice for yourself. What did you learn?

_____

_____

_____

_____

_____

Reading Plan and Observations

Read Luke 1–3. Use the space below to write down what you notice about Jesus and the Bible.

_____

_____

_____

_____

_____

_____

_____

_____

_____

_____

_____

_____

_____

_____

_____

_____

_____

_____

_____

Discussion

If you meet with a partner or group, study Luke 2:41–52 together. Discuss how Jesus points us to discipleship through diligent devotions. Use the space below to write about something you learn.

_____

_____

_____

_____

_____

_____

_____

_____

_____

_____

_____

_____

_____

_____

_____

_____

_____

~~~ 3 ~~~

RELIABLE RELATIONSHIPS

Prioritize the kind of relationships
that help you follow Jesus.

SHOW US YOUR CLOSEST FRIENDS, and we can determine
your spiritual condition. You may think that's an exaggeration,
but it's not. At every stage in your life, your companions will be
some of the most powerful influences. Their impact will either
help or hurt your discipleship, and their potential to reinforce
or redirect your devotion is undeniable. Your most consistent
friends will influence your most critical decisions.

That's why it is so important to surround yourself with godly
friends and mentors. It's challenging enough to walk with Jesus
in this world with them; don't attempt to do it alone. You need
other disciples to encourage you along the way. You must also
be aware of any negative influences rerouting God's direction
in your life.

Many young people can't continue on a path of discipleship because they surround themselves with friends going in
the opposite direction. If that statement makes you feel a bit
defensive, give us a moment. This challenge deserves your
attention. If you were walking down the street, you couldn't
physically walk in two directions at the same time. The same
is true spiritually. If Jesus is leading you one way and your
friends are pulling you the opposite way, you'll be forced to

make a decision. It's impossible to succeed in discipleship if your closest relationships disregard and discourage what Christ is inviting you to do.

Relationally Detached

Katie wasn't ready to start over at a new school, but changes in her family made it unavoidable. She didn't feel like she fit in, and none of the other kids showed interest in getting to know her. If the first few days in this city were any indication, she was going to have a long year. When an extended family member invited her to church, she wasn't thrilled at being ignored in another awkward environment. Eventually, she agreed to go to get the family member off her back.

What Katie found at the church's youth group was unlike anything she had ever experienced.

"Everyone is so nice! Do you do this every week? I can't wait to come back!" she told her family.

While Katie enjoyed the sermon, music, and games, she was changed by the students and adults who befriended her. Months later, she started following Jesus. Healthy relationships opened that door, and Katie knew she had to keep depending on those relationships in the church if she were to survive the challenges at home and school. They became the support system she needed.

Maybe you have your regular hangout crew who don't follow Jesus and then your church friends you see once or twice a week. That's not going to work for the long haul. The people who impact you the most are the ones you spend most of your time with. You won't find spiritual success if you have casual friends who follow the Word but best friends who follow the world.

You can't compartmentalize your life. It is impossible to follow Jesus without Him calling you to evaluate all aspects of who you are and what you do. That includes your relationships. If you are going to stay faithful in discipleship, your daily rhythms must include people who encourage you toward that goal.

You can't say, "Count me in," for discipleship if your most consistent companions say, "Count me out." If your closest friend always suggests you skip church, that will weigh on how much you are involved. If your boyfriend or girlfriend encourages you to break purity commands you know you should keep, you cannot endure such temptation for long. If your role models celebrate what God condemns, you will find yourself pursuing those same things.

But if your closest friends point you to your most important relationship with Christ, then the result is completely different. Their support will grow you in unthinkable ways—in the wisdom and favor we learned about in Luke 1–3. Having a heartfelt desire to follow Jesus is necessary, but you need to surround yourself with people who want to see that in you too.

If you took our advice in the last chapter and shared your Bible reading plan commitment with a partner, you probably can agree that action was helpful. Maybe you received the right type of encouragement at just the right time. Studying Scripture with someone else and sharing what you learn promotes deeper growth. When a mentor shares insights into how to study, it's an incredible gift. If you instead read the Bible on your own, consider: would you have reached the finish line in a better place if some like-minded people were running beside you?

We often share traits with the crowd we connect with most. Consider your group of friends. There's a good chance you wear the same style clothes. What about entertainment? Do you enjoy the same kind of music or media with your friends? If you spend enough time together, do you use the exact same phrases? That's normal. We all do it. Whoever occupies most of our time often shares most of our traits.

That's another reason your discipleship might not be where it should. You might not have a motivation problem or an opportunity issue. You have a *people* problem. You've probably felt the urge to grow, and you have numerous people and resources to help you do so. If you feel stuck, it could be the people around you are not supporting your desire for discipleship. No matter how passionate your intentions may be, your discipleship will be sabotaged if you allow your best friends to lead you to poor decisions.

Decide that the people closest to you will be closest to God. With them beside you, you will have the support you need to reach out to friends who don't know Jesus. Remember that whoever you are trying to influence might also be trying to influence you to another way of living. Establish a core group of friends who can keep you grounded in your discipleship, and then you will have the foundation to reach out to others.

Jesus and His Friends

Jesus knew reliable relationships were crucial to successful discipleship. His message and ministry highlight our need for each other.

Along with reading this chapter, you will study Jesus's commitment to twelve friends who literally changed the world in Luke 4-6. Although Jesus could have done all the work of ministry Himself, He invited twelve friends to join Him, and they were together consistently for three years.

Clarified Stances

God's Word has a way of clarifying stances. Once you hear it, you must determine if you are with God's ways or against them. For example, after Jesus successfully endured the devil's temptations (Luke 4:13), He began to minister in His hometown. News traveled fast about all Jesus was accomplishing (Luke 4:14-15). When He went to worship one day, He read Scripture that pointed to Himself. The people were furious. They didn't believe Jesus was the Messiah, so they literally tried to throw Him off a mountain. Those who should have seen Him clearest were blind to the truth before their eyes (Luke 4: 28-30).

Extreme relationships colored Jesus's entire life. Those who loved Him, loved Him deeply. Those who despised Him— they tried to kill Him. Jesus lived His life so clearly that no one could remain unclear on their relationship with Him. He shared God's path with anyone willing to listen. At the same time, He kept moving forward even when people rejected Him.

If you want a life where everyone loves you, you will quickly learn how impossible that is. If Jesus couldn't please everyone, neither can you. As you walk according to the Word, it will clarify people's stances. Some will want to embrace you as a friend, and others may want to throw you off a cliff. Respond like Jesus. Gather reliable friends, and keep moving forward—toward Jesus—no matter how many reject you.

Deep Relationships

One of Jesus's most famous disciples was a fisherman He nicknamed Peter. (His birth name was Simon.) Even before Jesus called Peter to follow Him, they were friends. How do we know? You typically only eat at the homes of people close to you, and in the Gospel of Luke, we find Jesus eating at Peter's house with his family.

Jesus was so close to Peter that Peter felt comfortable asking Jesus to help his mother-in-law, who was sick. Even Jesus's opponents knew who His friends were: the people with whom He ate (Luke 5:30).

You might be friendly with many people, but you can only be friends with a reasonable number. You likely have been to your closest friends' homes and know their family members by name. Those are signs of how close you are. For discipleship to be successful, you must be close to others, and that means seeing each other for more than an hour during a weekly Bible study. Relationships deepen when you connect throughout the week.

Close Proximity

You know you're tight with a friend when you can borrow their stuff. Jesus decided to borrow Peter's boat one day, but not for fishing. Jesus used it for preaching (Luke 5:3). As Peter cleaned his gear after an unsuccessful night of fishing (Luke 5:2, 5), he listened to Jesus preach and was in awe of the One using his boat as a pulpit.

Have you ever felt uncomfortable around someone who seemed so godly? Peter felt that in an extreme sense and asked Jesus to get away from him (Luke 5:8). Jesus was too holy, and Peter was too unholy. Instead of walking away from this confessing sinner, Jesus drew Peter closer. Jesus called Peter to follow Him and to join eleven other men who would work and live near Jesus (Luke 6:14-16). In response, Peter left the most profitable catch of his life to be in a more valuable relationship with Jesus (Luke 5:11).

People in reliable relationships are honest enough to share shortcomings but committed enough to stay despite them. We often don't want someone else to know the real us because of how they might respond. But relationships that nurture discipleship aren't scared off by our past failures or present struggles; they are motivated toward each other's future success. Jesus hasn't run off due to your sin. Neither should good friends. The most helpful friends are those who can acknowledge sin, highlight forgiveness, and encourage obedience.

Faithful Friends

As Jesus identified His friend group, they experienced ministry opportunities everywhere they went. They had plenty of stories to share about how God was working miracles. Not only had they seen them, but they also had a part in them. They were invited to the front row to observe Jesus's words and work and eventually participate.

One day, Jesus was teaching in a home. The crowd was so large that no one else could get through the door. While such a big crowd might have excited the disciples, it discouraged one group of friends.

The four men had heard about Jesus's miracles. They hoped He could heal their friend who was lame, and they weren't going to let a crowded room hold them back. They decided to remove a section of the roof and lower their friend into the room (Luke 5:19)! Jesus not only miraculously healed this man but also graciously forgave his sins.

What motivated Jesus to help? What moved Him to get involved? It wasn't the paralytic's faith. It was his friends' faith. "Seeing their faith he said, 'Friend, your sins are forgiven'" (Luke 5:20).

Did you catch it? Jesus was moved by the friends' faith! And, out of all the terms Jesus could have called the man in that moment, He called him, "Friend." The paralytic's friends' compassion moved Jesus, and Jesus befriended him as well.

Remarkably, Jesus calls us His friends (John 15:15). We are more than servants. We are friends with our Savior. He befriends us and encourages us to become friends with those who help us follow Him (John 15:17).

Circled Up

The paralyzed man was lowered into the house on a stretcher, but he walked out on his own, healed and forgiven. What caused such a dramatic change? His friends. They wouldn't stop until they got him to Jesus. We need those kinds of friends; we need to be those types of friends. No matter the cost and no matter the obstacles, we need friends who help us encounter the One who meets our deepest needs.

Who are the friends who would be at your side if you were down and out? We all long for steady companions who keep moving us forward no matter how difficult the challenges may be. But even if you have committed friends who will sit beside you when you are at your lowest, that doesn't guarantee they will help you get to the right places where you can find help.

Think about it: if the paralytic's friends had taken him to anyone other than Jesus, their compassion would have been wasted. The man wouldn't have gotten up and walked. He wouldn't have been forgiven of his sins or called "friend" by the Savior. That's why you need to consider the type of friends near you.

Sometimes the paralyzing situations we face are unexplained, and sometimes they are earned. You may face challenges you didn't ask for and can't overcome easily. It could be the loss of a family member, a challenge that makes school especially hard, or that annoying classmate who won't leave you alone. Those are challenging, but other situations could be the consequences of your actions. Maybe you've tried alcohol to fit in to the crowd, lied to your parents to hide bad grades, or let your anger out on someone close to you. In either case, well-intended yet misdirected friends won't help you take healthy and holy next steps.

If your soul's injuries are due to a bad habit or poor decisions, make sure your friends aren't trying to get you to return to the decisions that got you injured in the first place. You need compassionate friends with Christlike intentions. If your friends won't do everything in their power to get you to Jesus, you need to reconsider your friendships.

If your pool of solid friends is pretty shallow, first ask God to send the type of friends He wants in your life. Second, go to places where you'll find other people your age who follow Jesus. That's always a great start. Third, you will have to take some initiative. While you might hope everyone will come running up to talk with you, you might have to start a conversation. Fourth, be patient. Relationships take time. You don't stick first-time meetings in a spiritual microwave and expect deep relationships.

Count Me In for Reliable Relationships

As you study Luke 4–6, you will realize how intentional Jesus was in all His relationships, including those with the twelve disciples. He knew reliable relationships are vital to growth.

To build those relationships in your discipleship journey, take the following steps:

1. **GROUP.** Evaluate your existing relationships and their role in your discipleship. Who do you message the most? Who do you spend the most time with? Think about the people you are with regularly. Then, determine how helpful those people are. You don't have to remove all people from your life, but you might need to reprioritize their level of influence. As an exercise, list your friends in three groups: contagious disciples, potential believers, or unhelpful tempters. You may find you need to step away from some harmful relationships to step toward helpful ones.

2. **GATHER.** Once you establish a small number of people you want to keep close, decide when and where you will gather. Having a planned meeting helps create natural connections. Maybe you have a time your church has

set. If you feel that isn't enough, decide when you can meet at a coffee shop or somewhere after school.

The more detailed you are about the when and the where, the easier it will be to reach out for encouragement outside your regular rhythms. You might start gathering other disciples and sharing what you're learning through this study or praying for challenging situations. You could study a book of the Bible as well as learn what makes each of you tick. Getting to know each other better helps you know how to encourage each group member in his or her discipleship journey.

3. **GROW.** The more frequently you and your friends gather, the more you will grow in your relationship with Jesus and each other. Your friendship starts by accepting where each of you is spiritually but resisting the urge to stay in the same spot. Learn what motivates each other. Develop a strong friendship that knows where you are and where you need to be. If a mentor is available, even better. It is wonderful to have friends beside you and a mentor ahead of you.

In this next section of Luke, Jesus endured temptation by Himself (Luke 4:1). But on the eve of His crucifixion, Jesus drew the disciples to Himself and each other, warning them about their upcoming temptation (Luke 22:40).

As you continue your discipleship journey, don't go it alone. Nurture friendships with other disciples so you can strengthen each other when times get tough. Can we count you in for reliable relationships?

Insights

1. Which people in your life help you follow Jesus?

   _____

   _____

   _____

   _____

   _____

2. What relationships discourage your spiritual growth?

   _____

   _____

   _____

   _____

   _____

3. What traits in a friend help you the most?

   _____

   _____

   _____

   _____

   _____

4. How could you be a better friend to other disciples?

_____

_____

_____

_____

_____

5. List three ways a group of committed disciples could practically help each other.

_____

_____

_____

_____

_____

Reading Plan and Observations

Read Luke 4–6. While reading, write down what you notice about Jesus and His relationships.

_____

_____

_____

_____

_____

_____

_____

_____

_____

_____

_____

_____

_____

_____

_____

_____

_____

_____

_____

Discussion

If you meet with a group, study Luke 5:17–26. Discuss how Jesus points us to discipleship through reliable relationships. Use the space below to write about something you learn.

_____

_____

_____

_____

_____

_____

_____

_____

_____

_____

_____

_____

_____

_____

_____

_____

~ 4 ~

SELFLESS STANDARDS

*You will be disappointed with what this world
has to offer if you make it all about you.*

OVER AND OVER AGAIN, CULTURE tells us, "You be you!" But this encouragement rarely produces the results we want to see. What if "me being me" is the problem and not the solution? What if the change the world needs starts with self-denial instead of self-promotion?

If you always do what you want to do, you might find a moment of enjoyment, but it often creates long-term consequences. And, when you obey your urges, you often disobey God and damage others. If you were to evaluate your life honestly, your biggest regrets probably would be when you did what you wanted without thinking about how it would affect anyone or anything else. Listening to what we want and striving to be first is the worst thing we can do.

So here's our counter-cultural challenge: Don't be you. Be something better. Do something more: exhibit Christ *in* you. You do this by following His lead and embracing His selfless standards. When you put Jesus first and others second, you forget about yourself. Along the way, you'll find the real you, and surprise, surprise, you won't find it at the center of the universe.

Being a disciple of Jesus means you are a student of His ways. You can acknowledge that Jesus's path is far better than the ones you've been walking. You consider the words He said and the steps He took. Discipleship isn't you doing your own thing more successfully. It reroutes your perspective so that you do things differently, the way Jesus would.

Exhausting Pursuits

Anthony needed service hours for his school club, and his pastor gave him an opportunity to serve. As Anthony entered the doors of a ministry that helped kids with disabilities, he wasn't sure what he would do or how comfortable he would feel. But within minutes, he felt at ease and served above the baseline expectation. The kids loved him, and he loved the kids. He had such a great time that he invited some friends to come serve with him the following week.

The more Anthony served, the more he looked for other ways to help. People in his church commented to his parents that he seemed to be everywhere, helping out wherever there was a need.

Anthony's joyful willingness to do whatever was asked made a real difference. When the club recognized him for his service hours, he realized he had forgotten to put the last few weeks of volunteering on his paper. He enjoyed it so much that he had forgotten all about the credit. In many ways, he didn't want to be noticed for what he was doing. He considered it what a person ought to do as a follower of Jesus.

A selfless path is hard to envision. The world says only the strongest can survive, only the loudest can be heard, and only the best can be noticed. This pressure can cause you to over-achieve or underachieve. Both are exhausting.

Overachieving. If you compete with everyone clamoring for attention, you will work harder to be acknowledged and affirmed. You may shatter the current record, but someone better might be coming up behind you. Your social media post may gain you fifteen minutes of fame with the most likes you've ever received, but you will be forgotten when someone else's post goes viral. Your impressive physique and eye-catching looks may attract attention, but the stares and applause won't last forever. Working to be seen as better and smarter than others is an overwhelming, tiring pursuit.

Underachieving. If overachieving feels challenging, you might go to the other extreme: underachieving. It takes too much effort to stand out, so you decide to blend in. Underachieving tempts you to retreat to your room, detach from others, and neglect opportunities to do good in this world. This type of passivity is unhealthy. It's okay not to need everyone's constant attention, but you should live your life to draw attention to Jesus.

Although these two options are extremes, they have a common characteristic—pride. Both extremes set *you* at the center. The way of Jesus doesn't ask you to seek the limelight or to isolate yourself. Avoid the extremes of shining a light on yourself or failing to flicker on anything. Shine your light so that others see Jesus (Matthew 5:16).

Jesus and the Ministry

As we work on more selfless standards, we must look to Jesus, the model of selflessness. Your next reading in the Bible is Luke 7–9. In these chapters, Jesus's ministry is spreading rapidly, and needs arise everywhere.

As you read and study, notice how many of Jesus's ministry opportunities started as interruptions. He and His disciples would be walking somewhere, with an apparent agenda in mind, and people would stop Him, again and again, to ask for help. Through His example and encouragement, Jesus trained the disciples to put themselves last.

Worthy Opinions

One time, as Jesus entered a city, the Jewish leaders approached Him about a soldier's sick servant. This soldier had a significant role in their community. He had good character and even paid for their synagogue. The leaders believed this soldier was worthy of Jesus's attention (Luke 7:4). When Jesus heard the news, He went with them.

Even though the community thought the soldier was worthy of help, he considered himself unworthy. Yet the soldier knew Jesus could heal the sick servant just by speaking (Luke 7:7). The man was conflicted about asking Jesus to heal his servant. But Jesus's motivation to help had nothing to do with the soldier's reputation; Jesus was looking at the man's faith (Luke 7:9).

You will have an opportunity to help someone today. Someone will communicate a need to you, and you will have to decide—does this person deserve my attention? Is he or she worth my time? If you hesitate to help, you may value your personal freedom more than someone else's need. Jesus didn't allow opinions, expectations, or agendas to keep Him from doing good.

Compassionate Concern

In the same chapter of Luke, Jesus traveled farther down the road and encountered another need. This situation was worse than the first. Jesus didn't come upon another sick person; He came upon a funeral procession for a widow's only son (Luke 7:12).

Jesus never officially met these people. He wasn't in His hometown. Most people would walk by this procession and feel no responsibility whatsoever. Most people probably would avoid eye contact with the mother because of the pressure to say or do something.

But that's not how Jesus operated. He looked at the grieving widow and felt compassion for her (Luke 7:13). He didn't look around her. He didn't look past her. He didn't look through her. He looked *at* her. Jesus's compassion moved Him to bring the young man back to life. Jesus turned the funeral procession into a surprising celebration (Luke 7:16).

Have you ever looked around or past someone who needed help? What about that student who sits by himself? Do you know the story of that girl who always walks alone? In our hallways and on our highways, we avoid eye contact with those in need. But if we don't have our eyes on others, then our eyes are most likely fixed on ourselves. And when we're focused on ourselves, we can't see people's needs because we are too obsessed with our own.

Intentional Focus

Each time Jesus entered a city, He met a new set of needs. A religious leader named Jairus pleaded with Jesus to heal his twelve-year-old daughter who was dying (Luke 8:41). Jesus followed him, but on the way to Jairus's home, a woman struggling with sickness for twelve years sought healing (Luke 8:43–44). Her action stopped the procession. Jesus didn't mind. He stopped to talk to the timid woman. But what about Jairus? You can imagine Jairus frantically thinking, *Please hurry! My daughter is dying!*

Then Jesus said a name He is never recorded as saying in any other situation. *Daughter.* He healed the sick woman and called her daughter. "'Daughter,' he said to her, 'your faith has saved you. Go in peace'" (Luke 8:48). While one dad waited for the Savior to heal his daughter, the Savior made it clear He saw *all* needy women as daughters. It's a type of love that is difficult to explain. Jesus healed the woman's sickness and resurrected the man's daughter. He met both needs, but He also communicated a more profound truth that He lovingly cares for and addresses our weaknesses.

Both situations interrupted Jesus, but neither annoyed Him. The people's concerns became His agenda. Jesus didn't brush off their needs because He was too important. He addressed people's needs as if they were His family's needs. He didn't care if the person was an influential figure (Jairus) or a forgotten individual in the community (the woman).

To be more like Jesus, you must do the same. Stay alert to the needs around you, and treat hurting people with intentional focus. You will find freedom in being available to others instead of focusing on yourself.

It'll be hard; we oftentimes feel uncomfortable around people's pain and turn our attention away. The disciples felt the same way. In Luke 9, Jesus's disciples were overwhelmed by the number of hungry people who had come to hear Him speak. They had no plan to address that need and it wasn't their problem, so they tried to send the people away. But Jesus refused. He said, "You give them something to eat" (Luke 9:13). We cannot be Jesus's disciples and overlook the needs right in front of us. Jesus calls us to care and to act.

Self-Denial

As Jesus continued His ministry, He began preparing His disciples for His death (Luke 9:22). This teaching was not what they expected. The ministry was advancing, momentum was increasing, and support was rising. Why did Jesus ruin the mood by talking about something the disciples didn't want to even imagine was a possibility? Because Jesus had a goal greater than thriving in this world. He came to die for sinners. And through His death, a greater good would come.

Jesus's preparations defined and demonstrated what true discipleship should look like. "If anyone wants to follow after me," He said, "let him deny himself, take up his cross daily, and follow me. For whoever wants to save his life will lose it, but whoever loses his life because of me will save it. For what does it benefit someone if he gains the whole world, and yet loses or forfeits himself?" (Luke 9:23-25).

God made us so that our greatest joy is not found in self-focus but in self-denial. To do what God requires might mean giving up the things we desire, whether it's attention, comfort, free time, popularity, or convenience. You don't need to get everything you want. Just because it feels good doesn't mean you should do it. You must learn to delight in denial and realize that you are more than the summation of your feelings. If your desires disagree with God's biblical standards, you cannot blame God as if He made you to break His given commands. You will easily be entangled in certain temptations, but it is not because God made you that way.

In addition to saying we must deny ourselves, Jesus calls us to take up our crosses and lay down our lives. Jesus commanded this before His disciples saw Him hanging on a cross. When they heard Him say it, they had yet to hear "It is finished" on Golgotha or "He is risen" outside the empty tomb (John 19:30; Matthew 28:6). The cross was a public, humiliating execution. It was defeat. It was dreadful. It was death. And Jesus called them to take it up.

Give your life to Jesus, but not only once. Jesus says to take up our crosses *daily*. He calls us to daily die to self and live for Him. We can't follow Jesus and follow our hearts. We must make Him more important than our heartfelt desires and passionate pursuits.

Stepping Up

Jesus, the most importantly glorious person to ever walk this earth, refused to focus on Himself. You can't do the opposite and still live for Him. Following Jesus can't be littered with accepting invitations to veer off His path. Jesus offers a path toward self-denial, not self-discovery. He did not come to make your life better; He came to give you another life!

If such a claim seems too extreme, understand this: Discipleship is not an addition to your life. It is a replacement for the life you already have. It is stepping up to the life Jesus has designed you to live. If Jesus is only part of your story, you will step away from Him when His way is inconvenient and beg for His attention when consequences become unbearable. But

Jesus isn't meant to fit in as a part of your life. He is your life (Colossians 3:4)!

Following Jesus isn't an app you turn on in the church parking lot or when you need Him in a crisis. You will be increasingly disappointed, frustrated, and shallow if you follow Him that way. You must follow Jesus beyond church services, youth groups, and summer camps.

At home. Home is often one of the most challenging places to stay faithful. Since we know each other so well and have been through so much, we usually do our best for others and show our worst to our family. It is impossible to be a faithful disciple of Jesus while refusing to be selfless with your family members.

Are you willing to lay down what you want for what your family needs? You can honor your parents or guardians in how you take responsibility and show respect. You can serve your siblings by speaking encouragement more often than sarcasm. You can choose to highlight what's right instead of commenting on everything that's wrong.

With friends. Instead of requiring constant attention from your group of friends, be the friend who notices someone who needs a friend, recognizes when a friend is hurting, and focuses on others.

If and when your friendships have friction, be a source of reconciliation rather than further disagreement. Show righteousness instead of proving yourself right. If a relationship is strained, do what you can to improve it. In your friendships, follow Jesus and His example of selflessness.

By yourself. How do you follow Jesus when you're alone? Don't focus on yourself. Don't answer every selfish urge with sinful decisions. Don't waste every moment on unworthy distractions. Don't answer responsibility with procrastination.

Your discipleship journey will call you to stop doing certain things and start doing others. To avoid sin's traps, you will have to focus on holier pursuits. While your reputation is established through what people notice, your integrity is proven by what only God sees. The most telling indication of your discipleship is who you are and what you do when no one else is around.

Count Me In for Selfless Standards

Maintaining selfless standards throughout your life will be one of the most challenging yet rewarding decisions you can make. The more you become like Jesus, the more your service to others will be what you *get* to do rather than what you *have* to do. Life is more joyful and enjoyable when lived with a commitment to deny oneself.

Jesus's call to self-denial may seem challenging, but you can take some simple steps to see gradual change:

1. **HUMBLE.** You can only consider others more if you consider yourself less. God promises to humble those who exalt themselves but to exalt those who prioritize humility (Luke 14:11). Humility doesn't require looking down on yourself. It's looking away from yourself. Humility comes as you keep a proper perspective of who you are compared to Jesus, consider how He served others, and remove all barriers you have to living life humbly.

2. **HONOR.** Your words, actions, and expressions can either demean or honor others. If you try to outdo someone in any way, let it be in the way you honor them (Romans

12:10). Respect authority figures in your home, church, and school. Let your words encourage anyone who hears you (Ephesians 4:29). Follow Jesus's example in how you honor other people.

3. **HELP.** If you see a need, address it. Volunteer to help your parents around the house. Ask how you can help at church. Pay attention and be diligent when you are at school. Go the extra mile at your job. Give those you know best an extra dose of help. Jesus helped all kinds of people in all kinds of ways; let your selflessness be clear in how you help others.

Discipleship is more than sitting in a religious setting and thinking deeply. Discipleship takes what you are learning and looks for ways to live it out. Can we count you in for selfless standards? ·•*

Insights

1. Why do you think many teens struggle to be selfless?

   _____

   _____

   _____

   _____

   _____

2. What are three ways you can serve your family?

   _____

   _____

   _____

   _____

   _____

3. How can you reflect Christ by serving people at school or on your sports team?

   _____

   _____

   _____

   _____

   _____

4. How can you notice and encourage people instead of trying to be the one noticed and encouraged?

_____

_____

_____

_____

_____

5. What makes humbling ourselves easy compared to ways Jesus humbled Himself throughout His life?

_____

_____

_____

_____

_____

Reading Plan and Observations

Read Luke 7–9. While reading, write down what you notice about Jesus and the way He selflessly helped others.

_____

_____

_____

_____

_____

_____

_____

_____

_____

_____

_____

_____

_____

_____

_____

_____

_____

_____

Discussion

If you meet with a group, study Luke 9:23-27. Discuss how Jesus points us to discipleship through selfless standards. Use the space below to write about something you learn.

_____

_____

_____

_____

_____

_____

_____

_____

_____

_____

_____

_____

_____

_____

_____

_____

_____

_____

$\sim\sim$ **5** $\sim$

PERSISTENT PRAYER

Through prayer, you can talk with Jesus any
time, about anything, anywhere you are.

WHAT IF WE TOLD YOU that you have been given an incredible gift: immediate access to the most famous person in the world? That's right. You don't have to leave your house or even your bed to hear and be heard by that individual, no matter how much distance separates you. The connection is ready. The signal is strong. The opportunity is available. With a simple step, you can speak with the one person everyone craves to contact. Are you interested?

You wouldn't use your phone to make this connection. You'd use something more powerful. And you can probably guess we're not talking about communicating with a famous musician, inspiring athlete, or trending celebrity. We are talking about someone far more worthy. The gift is prayer, and the famous person is Jesus.

Through prayer, you can access Jesus any time, about anything, anywhere you are. Even though you are on earth and Jesus is in heaven, you will experience no dead zones in connection. No matter how often you pray, you will never drain the power supply. Through prayer, you come into Jesus's presence.

Unnecessarily Disconnected

Liz was used to acting like everything in her family was fine, but something changed one Sunday. Her small group leader asked for prayer requests, like every other week, and Liz opened up. She shared how her dad had made some poor decisions and her parents were planning to divorce. She asked for prayer, and the group responded. They prayed fervently, asking that God would get her dad's attention. The group kept praying throughout the week and continued to check on Liz.

A week later, they were amazed to hear that Liz's dad had come home, sought counseling, and apologized to the family for hurting them. Liz knew prayer worked in the Bible, but she had never seen it up close and personal. She never thought God would listen to someone like her, let alone act so obviously to help her. When she shared the changes that were happening in her family, her small group was overjoyed. They never took prayer requests lightly again.

Maybe prayer has seemed too abstract for you to give it serious attention. Maybe communicating with someone you can't see in front of you seems detached. But remember, all you've ever known is a world where phones constantly connect us with people we don't immediately see or hear. It's a blessing to be able to reach out from anywhere at anytime. And prayer is a much bigger blessing because the God of the universe is on the receiving end, and He always gets our messages—every worry and question and praise.

Prayer is our way of connecting with God, and it's the key for your discipleship to be successful. You need the Bible as your guide, good friends as your companions, and meaningful opportunities to serve, but prayer is the power that connects all these things together.

The longer you follow Jesus on the path of discipleship, the more consistently you will connect with Him through His Word and prayer. We primarily hear from God through Scripture and talk to God through prayer. Through prayer, you can talk with the most important person in the world about the most essential things in your life, and you can be reassured that He cares more than anyone else. Knowing God takes the time and attention to listen whenever you call out to Him is a gift. Tragically, the gift of prayer is too often avoided despite it being so readily accessible.

No doubt, prayer comes with challenges. Our minds wander. We doubt the effectiveness of things we can't see with our eyes. We might fear we're using the wrong words or structure to make our prayers "work."

But prayer is only as technical as you make it. Think about your closest friends. You know them well, so it's easy to talk with them. Now imagine you're sitting in a waiting room and stuck in small talk with a stranger. The conversation might seem awkward and forced.

That's why it's so important to get to know Jesus better. The more you know Him, the easier it is to talk with Him. You feel comfortable enough to be honest about how you are really doing. You discuss the things that burden you, because you believe they are important to Him. You even begin to process what is happening in your life through the filter of how He sees things.

Maybe you've only prayed when you were in trouble or overwhelmed by a particular set of circumstances—when you weren't ready for that big test, felt anxious about auditions, or worried about someone who was really sick. That's okay, but prayer can be so much more. For prayer to shift from an emergency call to a necessary ingredient in your discipleship, you must develop consistency. We always have things to pray about, and God is always available to listen. That's why persistent prayer must be a part of your discipleship strategy. Thankfully, Jesus showed and taught us a lot about how to pray.

Jesus and His Prayers

Jesus's life showed the power of prayer. He prioritized finding the space to pray in private and initiating the chance to pray in public. If the disciples couldn't find Jesus, they would search His favorite prayer spots.

In Luke 10–12, you'll discover how Jesus prioritized persistent prayer. You'll read how Jesus spent an entire night in prayer before He chose and called the twelve disciples (Luke 6:12). Since Jesus is the Son of God, He could have made those decisions without losing sleep or prolonged prayer. But Jesus prayed all night. Why? Not because He didn't know what to do in a big decision, but because we could benefit from His example of focused prayer times when we have a major need for God's guidance. His prayer life wasn't a personal requirement so much as it was a generous example.

Prayerful Focus

You've read about Jesus's twelve disciples ("learners"), who were with Him all the time. He later called them apostles ("sent out ones") (Luke 6:13). The change in name signified they would transition from learners to doers. Jesus brought them close to send them out.

In addition to these twelve, Jesus had many other disciples or students. They weren't around as much as the twelve, but they grew spiritually during their time with Jesus. At some point in Jesus's ministry, He sent out seventy-two disciples to do what they had seen Him do. Paired up, these disciples were to travel to different communities and prepare the way for Jesus's ministry. Before sending them off, Jesus didn't tell them to train, strategize, or mobilize. Instead, He urged the disciples to pray (Luke 10:2). Knowing the job would be difficult, Jesus told them to ask God for more workers rather than relying on their own strength.

Even though these disciples had spent years with Jesus, they needed prayer as they headed out on their own. The strategy apparently worked because, once they returned, Jesus said their work had rattled the devil's efforts (Luke 10:18). Don't miss this truth for your own discipleship. You will never rise to a level where you don't need to pray. If you want to see God do amazing things through your life, ask Him to do it rather than relying on your own strength.

Prayerful Template

As these disciples watched Jesus live every hour of His life for the glory of God and the good of others, they were mesmerized. The more wonders they saw Jesus do, the more opportunities He gave them to do the same type of work. They must have felt the need for some serious tutorials. But after all they had seen and heard, they didn't ask Jesus for a lesson on how to heal a sickness, feed a crowd, or raise the dead. They asked Him how to pray (Luke 11:1).

His response provided what we call "The Lord's Prayer." Many people memorize it, and some churches recite it, but Jesus provided the words as more of a template than a script. Yes, the prayer is helpful to speak from memory, but it's even better as a guide for prayer.

If your prayers have ever felt stuck on repeat, I've got good news for you—they don't have to stay that way. Use Jesus's prayer as an example to fuel your own (Luke 11:2–4). Instead of starting with a long list of personal requests, begin in worship ("Your name be honored as holy"). Then move to surrender ("Your kingdom come"), transition to request ("give us each day our daily bread"), pivot to confession ("forgive us our sins"), and end with protection ("do not bring us into temptation").

Worrisome Responses

Jesus had this unbelievable way of taking God's truth and applying it to people's everyday lives. From His teaching, it sounds as if anxiety was a widespread phenomenon. Many people worried about what they would eat or wear (Luke 12:22). Such concerns, back then and now, can cause people to become increasingly anxious, which can lead to frantically trying to address personal needs and wants.

When we are anxious, Jesus encourages us to seek His kingdom and to tell God our Father (Luke 12:31). God knows what we need even before we ask Him (Luke 12:30). Jesus's encouragement is more than a spiritual saying. It should be our active pursuit. Don't let hard or worrisome situations drive you to fear, worry, and complain; let them lead you to seek God's kingdom through prayer.

Do you struggle with anxiety? Let's rephrase that. *How* do you struggle with anxiety? All of us worry about some things but process them in different ways. This world provides numerous reasons to make us fearful, so we need a plan for handling our anxious feelings. According to Jesus, acting as if you don't have concerns does not prove strength. He said that God knows our needs and cares about us (Luke 12:30). Don't believe that admitting your struggles in prayer makes you appear weak. That can't be true if Jesus tells you to do just that.

What are your concerns right now? It doesn't matter how big or small they are. Through prayer, you can talk to God about the most essential things in your life and trust that He knows what to do with them.

Continuous Requests

God invites you to call Him "Father" (Luke 11:2). When you pray, you aren't speaking to a distant God somewhere in the sky. You are calling out to your consistently near Father, who knows exactly what you need (Luke 12:30).

Jesus once told a story about a persistent friend. This friend woke up a neighbor in the middle of the night to ask for some bread. Annoyed by the request, the neighbor eventually gave his friend what was needed so that he could go back to bed (Luke 11:8). The friend received what he wanted because he kept asking until his need was met.

You might find this story odd, but Jesus is teaching something important. He isn't implying God gives up and provides us what we want if we repeatedly irritate Him until He surrenders.

He's saying that if impatient neighbors will relent due to a friend's consistent pressure, how much more can we trust a loving Father to rise and meet our needs? "If you then, who are evil, know how to give good gifts to your children, how much more will the heavenly Father give the Holy Spirit to those who ask him?" (Luke 11:13).

We often don't have what we need because we fail to ask. Jesus said we miss wonderful opportunities in life when we fail to pray: "So I say to you, ask, and it will be given to you. Seek, and you will find. Knock, and the door will be opened to you" (Luke 11:9). Prayer is going to the door of God's house, knowing our Father isn't frustrated or annoyed by our requests. He welcomes them. Through prayer, we knock on God's door, and He invites us in to enjoy all the blessings He makes available to us.

Looking Up

Prayer was not something Jesus did when He got around to it. He set aside time and space to pray. His example shows prayer is essential to making it through all we encounter. We don't know what we will experience next, so we must stay connected to the One who can guide us through anything and everything.

Prayer is God's invitation to look up. Instead of looking into a mirror for help, we gaze toward our heavenly Father, who is far more capable than we are. The more we rely on ourselves, the more discouraged we will become. But the more we pray to God, the more reliable He proves to be. Prayer can become a habit because, the more you practice it, the more you realize its power.

Of all the names Jesus could have taught us to use when praying, He encouraged us to approach God as our heavenly Father. Both parts of that name are significant. He is our Father, which proves He is near. He is concerned about our well-being and is the only One who knows what is best. At the same time, our Father resides in heaven. Of all the places our Father could reside, His address is heaven. That means nothing is too difficult for Him. Nothing we could ever ask could be outside of His ability to accomplish.

God is your Father, and you are His kid. No matter what you have to say, you can talk with Him. There is no need to be afraid. And just like you get comfortable with someone by hanging around that person, the same is true of God. How do you learn to pray? You learn to pray by praying. The more you pray, the easier it becomes. Don't worry about saying the wrong thing because God knows your heart.

You may have experienced that awkward silence in church when someone asks, "Does anyone want to lead us in prayer?" Most in the room hope someone else will rise to the challenge. The pressure continues to mount until someone finally volunteers. For many people, leading a group in prayer can be nerve-racking. Here's a way to work on that fear: the more we pray in secret, the easier it is to pray in public.

Make prayer such a consistent habit that you pursue it alone and in a group. Prayer is intended to remove fear, not increase it. If we stopped worrying about what others thought and instead received prayer as the gift that it is, maybe no one would have to ask us to pray. We wouldn't be able to go long without it.

Count Me In for Persistent Prayer

No discipleship journey is complete without a commitment to persistent prayer. This connection with God empowers all the other components of following Jesus. As you journey on, here are some ways to prioritize persistent prayer:

1. **SCHEDULE.** You're more likely to pray if you put it on your calendar. Schedule prayer somewhere during your day so that you treat it as you would a meetup with any other significant person in your life. The more often you keep scheduled times to pray, the easier it will be for spontaneous prayer times to happen.

2. **SECLUDE.** Do everything you can to remove distractions as you attempt to pray. Don't have electronic devices within your reach. Find a quiet place with fewer chances of interruptions. You might find that physically kneeling helps you keep your spiritual focus. Or if walking while praying helps, do that! Find whatever keeps you focused.

3. **SWITCH.** Don't pray about the same thing every time you talk to God. Switch it up! If you repeatedly say the same things to your best friend, you get bored with one another, and the relationship dissolves. Make a list of different people and situations to pray for every day of the week so that your prayers remain varied. Writing them down and having a daily focus also will help you stay alert to how God answers your requests.

4. **SPEAK.** Whenever possible, pray out loud. This suggestion may seem unique, but it really helps. All of us

struggle with daydreaming, and when we pray with our minds and not our lips, we become even more prone to mindlessly drifting. We switch back and forth between thinking and praying and eventually give up. Even if you don't want to bother other people or have to be quiet, try whispering your prayers. It is more difficult to be distracted when you verbalize your prayers.

Prayer is a gift. It connects us to the most glorious One in all the universe. He is not annoyed by your requests. He invites you to come to Him anytime, with anything. Can we count you in for persistent prayer?

Insights

1. Can you name three things that keep you from spending time in prayer?

   _____

   _____

   _____

   _____

   _____

2. Have you ever seen prayer work in your life? Write down those times.

   _____

   _____

   _____

   _____

   _____

3. What do you think God thinks about you when you call out to Him?

   _____

   _____

   _____

   _____

4. Look at your answer to question 3. How does it compare to Jesus's description of God as a Father who waits on our requests (see Luke 11:13)?

_____

_____

_____

_____

_____

5. What are the greatest needs in your life right now? When will you schedule a time to pray for them?

_____

_____

_____

_____

_____

Reading Plan and Observations

Read Luke 10–12. As you read, write down what you notice about Jesus and prayer.

_____

_____

_____

_____

_____

_____

_____

_____

_____

_____

_____

_____

_____

_____

_____

_____

_____

_____

_____

_____

_____

_____

Discussion

If you meet with a group, study Luke 11:1–13. Discuss how Jesus points us to discipleship through persistent prayer. Use the space below to write about something you learn.

_____

_____

_____

_____

_____

_____

_____

_____

_____

_____

_____

_____

_____

_____

_____

_____

_____

_____

_____

$\sim\!\!\sim$ 6 $\sim\!\!\sim$

GRADUAL GROWTH

It's hard to see progress if you never define
what you are working toward.

SOME THINGS IN LIFE REQUIRE effort. You won't earn a diploma simply by driving into a school parking lot. A team won't win the state championship by putting gear in a locker room and waiting for a trophy to arrive. Your family will never get to that summer vacation until someone puts it on the calendar and packs the suitcases. It sounds simple, right? In all areas of life, opportunities don't necessarily lead to success. Degrees are earned by showing up for class and putting in the work. Championships are awarded to those who commit to the gym and compete in the game. Vacations are enjoyed by those who get in the car and drive to the destination. What's the common factor in these examples? Effort and plans. Getting where we want to be requires both these things.

Why don't we consider that regarding discipleship? Do we think that showing up at church with no plan and no effort will somehow turn us into a mature disciple of Christ? It just won't work.

To grow like we ought to grow, we must develop a clear plan. It is a path of dedicated discipleship. It is a refusal to be directionless in our following of Jesus. If you say you want to develop in discipleship but can't clearly define what areas you need to work on, you may find yourself stuck. You can have all the passion in the world, but it is pointless if you don't know what it is driving you to do.

Neglecting Plans

"So what happens now?" Ben asked.

His question was sincere. He had become a Christian and signed up to be baptized. He wanted to know if there was something else he was supposed to do. His dad's response was not what he expected.

"Well," said Ben's dad, "we are actually just getting started. Now, I get to disciple you."

Ben thought disciples were just those guys who followed Jesus around, but his dad was inviting him into the same process. Ben's dad had a simple strategy: to take everything he knew, share it with his son, and expect his son to share it with someone else. As Ben grew in the faith, he and his dad prioritized specific things for Ben to work on.

You will benefit greatly if you develop a discipleship growth plan. Maybe you thought that's what this book would do for you. You're partially right. This book will give you some of the tools you need to establish and continue your discipleship plan long after you close it. Basically, it'll jump-start your discipleship process, but it won't take you to complete spiritual maturity by the last page. Our hope is that this book will encourage you to keep growing and maturing until your last day.

Discipleship is often a weird concept to many Christians. The last thing Jesus told His disciples to do was to make disciples of all nations (Matthew 28:18–20). Salvation is not a finish line of God's work in your life but the starting line of lifelong discipleship. Many people think they've arrived the moment they tell others they are ready to become a Christian. Yes, that's a crucial step, but it cannot be the last. If all Jesus asked you to do was believe Him, you could move on once you checked that box. Jesus calls you to follow Him, not just believe Him. To follow Jesus, you must move in a clear direction toward Him.

Here's what is unique about your discipleship journey: no one else is in the same spot as you. Think about the need for persistent prayer in a disciple's life. Do we all need to be people of prayer? Of course we do. Is everyone at the same level of consistency in their prayers? Absolutely not! No two individuals are alike or need the same directions for their discipleship journey. A good resource on any given topic can help anyone, but we all need more specific instructions for our unique situations.

If each of us is in a different stage of discipleship, how do you know what to do next? First, you must determine where you are spiritually. Honestly evaluating how healthy you are is a good start. How consistent are your spiritual habits, such as reading the Bible, spending time in prayer, or meeting with other Christians? What sin trips you up again and again? Is there a bad habit you wish you didn't have excuses for anymore but rather a plan for progress? Identifying where you are helps you thank God for how far He has brought you while looking toward where He wants to take you.

Second, you must clarify where you hope to be soon. What's your end goal? Define the direction. Once you establish your destination, make a plan and take the necessary turns to get there. You may want to discard bad habits and replace them with good ones. Maybe it's time to put down the device and pick up the Bible. Have you thought about how you could go to church and serve people? Perhaps you might finally volunteer for that mission opportunity you kept saying you weren't ready for.

You won't get where you want to go by accident. You won't stumble into church or fall into discipleship. What if you decided to evaluate where you are and made a plan to reach your goal?

Jesus and the Cost

When Jesus called His disciples to follow Him, He encouraged them to unfollow other things. He wanted first place in their lives. For His disciples who were fishermen, taking up a cross meant laying down a net.

Jesus never made it easy to follow Him. He knew people would come for the perks—the healings, the teaching, the food—but leave when given the tasks. He never lowered the bar, though, or used false advertising. He didn't hide the need for personal effort. To follow Jesus meant to walk down a path where you wouldn't have to worry about bumping into many others. The path to gradual growth and discipleship isn't crowded.

Narrowed Focus

As Jesus's reputation grew, so did the crowds as He entered a new region or town. People wanted to see Jesus up close and personal, but they really came to see what He would do for them. That's what made one of His descriptions of discipleship so shocking. "Make every effort to enter through the narrow door, because I tell you, many will try to enter and won't be able" (Luke 13:24).

Jesus understood some people came for the show. But others followed Him for more than what He could do for them. Since Jesus knew people's hearts, He understood how many would miss the correct path. He knew a day was coming when many would be shocked they weren't welcomed at the heavenly door. They experienced religious fellowship and heard biblical preaching (Luke 13:26)—how was that not enough? Jesus said that although their spiritual lives looked busy, they were never in a relationship with Him (Luke 13:27).

You may know people who come for the religious show. They attend church when nothing else is on the calendar. They attend the fun activities but never commit to the volunteer service. It is possible to associate with Jesus without ever entering a relationship with Him. Discipleship moves people from knowing about Jesus to knowing Jesus.

Humble Attitude

While visiting a house filled with influential community members one day, Jesus told a parable about humility. A parable is a short, memorable story that illustrates a spiritual truth. Jesus was a master storyteller. He told His listeners that when they were invited to a wedding banquet, they should not take the best seat. It would be embarrassing if someone more important came and the host wanted to switch seating arrangements (Luke 14:8–9). Jesus said it was better to take the worst seat and let the host move you up if he saw fit (Luke 14:10–11).

Can you imagine the awkward feeling in the room as Jesus spoke? He was in a house with people who likely tried to get the most distinguished seats as near to the most popular people in the room as possible, but Jesus was criticizing such practices.

What does this parable teach us about discipleship? Only humble people can admit they aren't the most influential in the room. If you value others more than yourself, you have positioned yourself to serve and learn from others. You are ready to say "no" to yourself and "yes" to Jesus. But if you walk into every room expecting others to move out of their way to honor you, you have missed the path of discipleship. Seeking to be first reveals you should be last.

Accepted Invitation

Jesus told another parable. A wealthy man sent invitations for an impressive banquet (Luke 14:16). As the servants delivered the message, they surely anticipated a great response. But instead of gratefully receiving the gracious invitations, the people made excuses for why they couldn't come (Luke 14:18).

One had a new piece of land to survey, another purchased some livestock to evaluate, and another prioritized spending time with his wife (Luke 14:18-20). None of those things were evil. But the people's priorities showed they were so committed to other things that they couldn't see the invitation's value.

When it comes to Jesus's invitation to be His disciple, have you assessed the offer on the table? It is more valuable than anything this world has to offer. How could you pass it up? You will only refuse the invitation to discipleship if you value something more. Your excuses might be similar to those in Jesus's parables. Would you rather focus on a pursuit, purchase, or person more than Jesus? If so, you will never get around to discipleship. You might succeed in school, impress people with all your gadgets, or provoke jealousy with your relationships, but none of those things are worth it if you miss Jesus in the process.

Evaluated Cost

The invitation to follow Jesus came with a cost. He told His followers He must come first. If they deemed someone more important, they would feel the tug to walk away. Their level of commitment to Jesus should make all other relationships pale in comparison (Luke 14:26). Jesus used strong wording to highlight how their level of allegiance to Him must be unmistakable to others.

Committing to being a disciple of Jesus means counting the cost and dying to the possibility of anything else taking first place (Luke 14:27). Jesus then illustrated how plans revealed commitments with more word pictures. If you were building a tower, you would first make sure you had enough money to purchase all the construction materials (Luke 14:28). If you were engaging in a battle, you would first configure your troops for the best chance of success (Luke 14:31). If you wouldn't build a tower without a plan, then why do you try to grow spiritually without any blueprint? If you wouldn't wage a battle without a strategy and support, how do you plan to face an enemy who has both in place?

So much of our work is left undone and so many of us walk away from battles defeated because we never evaluated the cost. Once you set a goal of where you want to be, you must consider and assemble the components necessary to getting there. Make sure you have the right tools. Seek out experts when questions arise. Surround yourself with people who can help you complete the task.

So what do you plan to build? Where do you want to go? What battle do you intend to fight? Jesus's examples are eye-opening. Discipleship often includes things we need to create and things we need to discard. Ask yourself: *What needs to be developed? What needs to be destroyed?*

Growing Up

Making necessary changes takes maturity and diligence. You will have to start seeing yourself as capable, growing, and maturing. You will also have to be persistent in making those changes happen through goals, plans, and routines.

Can you imagine your school suddenly saying naptime would be part of the school day? If the teacher lowered the lights, passed out baby bottles, and rolled out mats, that would definitely change the feel of the school. Nothing is wrong with those practices, but they are meant for very young children. You should no longer need them. If you did, people would think you needed more than a nap.

That naptime illustration shows how we should grow up and mature. The apostle Paul said he "put aside childish things" (1 Corinthians 13:11). If you don't need a baby's schedule because you've outgrown it, what have you moved past in your spiritual journey? Is your progress observable?

The Bible characterizes spiritually underdeveloped people as infants wanting milk rather than solid food (Hebrews 5:12). It is a picture of how some people who should be sitting at the table still require a highchair. We can't stay in a state of spiritual infancy. We must grow up!

Teens have amazing potential. You have passion and energy that many adults envy. Use them to ensure maturity follows. If you were to harness your drive with gradual and continual growth, who knows all you could experience?

Maintain your youthful energy but mature past childlike ways. Don't eliminate your vibrance; enhance your reliability. Find Christian mentors you desire to imitate. Find the most contagious Christians you know, and learn from them. We all learned to do simple and complex things by watching people further along than us. The same is true in discipleship.

Count Me In for Gradual Growth

At your age, you know what it's like to fear the future while feeling confident about what you've already made it through. Maybe you're nervous when you think about applying for college, but you no longer worry about how to give a presentation in history class. You can learn from the upperclassmen and teach the underclassmen. At every turn, what seemed impossible from afar becomes possible when you are in it.

Discipleship works the same way. You should not only learn from those ahead of you but also teach those behind you. What seems difficult is more attainable than you can imagine. You simply need to learn from people who are further along than you. But don't forget those behind you. They're wondering if they can do what you make look easy. They can if you teach them! Part of growing up—in general and as Jesus's disciple—is accepting the next challenge and bringing someone with you.

Do you remember how nervous you were the first day at your school? After a few weeks, you could get to class without thinking about it. You knew how to find your friends and understood how your schedule worked. After discovering a plan, you had what you needed to succeed. Similarly, your discipleship plan ensures you have the people and resources necessary to stay on Jesus's path. It can even become something you pass on to someone else. Here are some ways to continue your gradual growth in discipleship:

1. **IMITATE.** Paul told a church that if they wanted to follow Jesus, they should start by following Paul (1 Corinthians 11:1). That might sound conceited, but he was outlining the path of discipleship. A more mature disciple invites a less mature disciple to follow Jesus together. Whose faith do you want to replicate? Do you see a contagious lifestyle for Jesus that you wish you had? Stick with that person. Ask him or her to disciple you. Learn everything you can.

2. **IDENTIFY.** As you work with your mentor, develop a plan for how you need to grow. Identify what needs to be built and what needs to be destroyed, and detail a plan for how you will go about it. Then, notice your progress as you follow your individualized discipleship plan.

3. **INVEST.** Don't wait to feel mature before investing in someone else. Do you know why? You'll never get to full maturity this side of heaven. When we make an imaginary line of what we need to know and do before we make another disciple, we typically find the line moves as we get closer to it. You have spiritual knowledge and

life experience that someone else needs. Take all that you have and share it with someone else.

Jesus is calling you to follow Him. You'll need to take some turns along the way to get where He is leading you. But don't worry—He has provided His Word as your direction, the Holy Spirit as your guide, and other believers as your companions on the journey. Can we count you in for gradual growth?

Insights

1. Are you someone who makes plans easily? Why or why not?

   _____

   _____

   _____

   _____

   _____

2. What part of your discipleship journey needs to grow and develop?

   _____

   _____

   _____

   _____

   _____

3. What needs to be destroyed to help you follow Jesus better?

   _____

   _____

   _____

   _____

4. Who is someone you wish would disciple you?

_____

_____

_____

_____

_____

5. Who is someone you could disciple?

_____

_____

_____

_____

_____

Reading Plan and Observations

Read Luke 13–15. While reading, write down what Jesus says about gradually growing in discipleship.

_____

_____

_____

_____

_____

_____

_____

_____

_____

_____

_____

_____

_____

_____

_____

_____

_____

_____

_____

Discussion

If you meet with a group, study Luke 14:25–33 together. Discuss how Jesus points us to gradual yet continual growth. Use the space below to write about something you learn.

_____

_____

_____

_____

_____

_____

_____

_____

_____

_____

_____

_____

_____

_____

_____

_____

_____

~~~ **7** ~~~

COUNTERCULTURAL CONTENTMENT

*You have everything you need even when
you don't have everything you want.*

EVERYWHERE YOU GO, YOU'RE BOMBARDED with a repeated
message: you don't have enough. It's a dangerous implica-
tion. It suggests you aren't enough if you don't own enough.
That group of friends won't accept you until you get what they
have. Your new purchase is already outdated, so you need an
upgrade. From ads and online influencers to what people flaunt
in person, you have to fight to stay content and stop wishing
for more, more, more.

No matter how blessed you think you are, it's hard to remain
content when you're constantly reminded of what you don't
have. You probably want the newest phone everyone is talking
about, and you might feel jealous of the attention your friends
or classmates get when they have the latest clothes or the
trendiest car. These feelings can cause you to overlook your
blessings, to resent your family for not giving you what you
want, or to make poor decisions. The stuff you *want* begins to
feel like stuff you *need*.

A big part of discipleship is learning to deal with the messages and things of this world. Heaven is at stake, but we will
settle for earthly pursuits if we don't keep our materialism in
check.

Richly Unaware

Brian didn't mean to upset his classmate, but he did. As he gathered with a group of guys after Christmas break, they began sharing the impressive gifts they had received. Brian said he wasn't sure he had enough room for the tons and tons of presents he had unwrapped.

He wasn't prepared for his new friend Trey to turn and walk away, saying, "Wow. I wish I just had a home."

Brian didn't know Trey's family was in turmoil. He had no idea Trey slept in an unfamiliar place, overseen by new caretakers, without a bed to call his own. When Brian went home that day, he looked at all his gifts differently. He even looked at his room with a different appreciation than before.

You might be on one of those extremes. Maybe you have everything you need and more, or perhaps you have a long list of needs. Regardless of how much or how little you have, being grateful is a helpful quality. Even if you have a lot, someone probably has more than you. Even if you are in a tight spot, someone in this world is in worse condition.

Why is that important to remember? You may not have everything you want, but God has provided for your needs. Even if you haven't thought about it in a while, you are probably more blessed than you think. Suppose you have running water, wireless internet, heating and air conditioning, and a printed book in your language. If so, you're already wealthier than most people in the world!

It might feel weird to make a big deal about those things. It's easy to take them for granted. That's the point. We need to think about our everyday blessings more often.

When we do, we more often remember to thank God for what He has given. When we don't, we can become obsessed with wanting what others have. We begin to believe something is wrong with us until we have the same clothes, devices, car, and status as our friends. That type of thinking will get your focus off your spiritual condition and onto your physical comforts. Nothing can slow down your discipleship growth as quickly as a discontented heart that's pursuing what this world says is important.

Envy is normal. It's a real struggle not to be envious when you see all this world has to offer. But we want to warn you against materialism, the love of money and creature comforts. It has dulled many eager disciples along the way. Don't be distracted by what this world offers. None of it, not even the best and brightest, is as valuable as what Christ offers you.

Jesus and Possessions

In Luke 16–18, Jesus declared and demonstrated how countercultural contentment relates to discipleship. He talked about money and possessions repeatedly. And, even with the wealth of heaven at His fingertips, Jesus chose to live His days as a wandering homeless man, dependent upon others for meals and places to sleep. His detachment from the things of this world allowed Him to focus on more important matters.

If His example seems countercultural now, know it was just as shocking then. People were uncomfortable with Jesus's stance on possessions. In His culture, people's status was determined by how much they owned. Yet Jesus never caved to the wealthy or dismissed the poor.

Loving Money

The Pharisees (the religious leaders of the day) disliked Jesus. His sermons opposed many of their practices. Luke tells us these leaders loved money (Luke 16:14), which Jesus spoke against. It makes sense that these leaders despised someone who encouraged them to think of getting rich less and to think about others more.

Jesus saw a correlation between how the Pharisees handled material goods and how they prioritized spiritual matters. "No servant can serve two masters," He said, "since either he will hate one and love the other, or he will be devoted to one and despise the other. You cannot serve both God and money" (Luke 16:13). Jesus was calling them to decide who would have first place in their lives.

You are no different. You cannot say Jesus is Lord and be obsessed with getting stuff. If you want something fervently enough—even though Jesus says you don't need it—you will be tempted to turn from Him. When you make possessions more important than Jesus, you slow down your discipleship and block yourself from growth.

Considering Eternity

Jesus illustrated His point about the love of money with a parable about a rich man and a poor man. The rich man enjoyed all the finest things. The poor man suffered poverty and sickness. He was so poor and hungry that he longed to eat what fell off the rich man's table (Luke 16:21).

You might feel bad for the poor man, and rightly so. Jesus's story, though, takes a surprising turn. He fast-forwards to the time after the two men die. The poor man was spending eternity with God while the rich man was not. Their positions had swapped dramatically, but what's worth considering is the length of time each man suffered. While on earth, the poor man's suffering probably felt like an eternity, but that was nothing compared to the rich man's actual eternity (Luke 16:24).

Jesus emphasized a critical point to consider. What we have in this life is not what we will experience in eternity. Even if you spend your years on earth without a ton of possessions, those worldly things can't compare to the heavenly experiences you will enjoy forever. The alternate is true as well. If you spend an eternity away from God, you won't be comforted by thinking, *Well, at least I had those glory days on earth with all my nice stuff.*

Seeking Security

Speaking of eternity, Jesus told His listeners a day was coming when He would return. The things of earth would be eliminated, and the final reality would begin. Many people wanted to know when that day would be. If they could put it on their calendar, they could fill their days with earthly wants and cram in eternal matters at the last minute.

Jesus refused to give a timeline, although He did provide some warnings. This world won't last forever, and all its entertainments and distractions won't either. Jesus even pointed out that people would be buying and selling things when He returned, oblivious to higher matters (Luke 17:28). If we live our days carefree and never prepare for our last ones, we will suddenly have no more time to address our spiritual condition. "Whoever tries to make his life secure will lose it, and whoever loses his life will preserve it" (Luke 17:33).

At your age, it may be hard to think about Jesus's return in such abstract terms. Visualizing what life will be like in college is challenging enough. Comprehending Jesus's return to earth in the last days seems even harder to imagine. Although His return may not consume your thoughts, you do need to consider it. You must also realize you can't find security in the stuff you earn or purchase. In a very materialistic culture, you need to take an honest look at deeper issues. Jesus constantly reminds us that our lives and eternity are more important than how much stuff we get.

Making Decisions

One day, an impressive young man asked Jesus what he needed to do to guarantee eternal life (Luke 18:18). The man was successful for someone his age and had been religious since he was a child.

After listening to the young man, Jesus offered an invitation that would reveal the man's heart: "Sell all you have and distribute it to the poor, and you will have treasure in heaven. Then come, follow me" (Luke 18:22). The man walked away. His love of possessions was bigger than his concern about his eternal state.

You may not be in the same situation as this guy, but you probably have some similarities. You're young, and you're probably richer than many people in the world.

Also, like this young man, you have a choice to make. Will you let the things of this world numb you to the things that will remain once this world is gone? Jesus said it is incredibly challenging for self-sufficient, self-reliant, worldly obsessed people to go to heaven because they don't see their need for it

(Luke 18:25). They believe that money can buy them anything. They think the rules don't apply the same to them. It is easy for wealthy people to assume they have no need for God.

Jesus didn't command everyone to sell their possessions to follow Him, but He did give this instruction to the young man. Why? The man's possessions had a hold on him that would keep him from discipleship. It's not evil to have stuff, but material goods must have the right priority. You can own things as long as they don't own you. For those of us who choose discipleship over wealth, Jesus says our reward will far transcend anything this world offers (Luke 18:30).

Giving Up

What can block the type of contentment Jesus calls us to embrace? One thing is blindness. We will never be content if we can't see how blessed we are. Another is listening to the urge to acquire more. We must give up pursuing everything this world says is essential.

Stuff can't save us. The world's focus on getting more stuff is a false gospel. The true gospel is the good news of what Jesus has done. Its hopeful announcement goes like this:

1. God is the ideal, a loving and compassionate Creator.
2. We wrongly rebelled against God, rejecting His gifts, and demanding what we thought we deserved.
3. Jesus addressed our sins by dying for us on the cross.

4. Now we can follow Him and experience the peace we so desperately need.

The gospel tells us what is ideal, what went wrong, how to fix it, and where it's all going.

That's why the pursuit of possessions is a false gospel. Here's the world's version:

1. The ideal life is having everything you want.
2. What's wrong with you is the fact that you don't have what others have.
3. You can fix the wrongness by getting more stuff, even if it requires stealing, borrowing, or begging so others can respect your status.
4. When you do, you'll get to a place where you can live impressively so that others respect and envy you.

Every step of the world's gospel is wrong. More stuff won't fix what's broken in this world and in our hearts. We can't make heaven here on earth. We need something more valuable than the latest product; we need to give up on the way of this world and develop hope in the countercultural ways of the one to come. God has given us more than we deserve, and we are blessed more than we can imagine.

Once we know that Jesus addresses our most profound issues, we don't have to be distracted by lesser concerns. Jesus loves us, with or without the hot items flying off the shelves. We don't need the stuff of this world because we have the guarantee of the one to come. This world thinks that all that glitters is gold, but God uses gold to pave the streets in heaven (Revelation 21:21). Doesn't that prove how much better that home will be? The stuff we crave to hold up for all to see in this world will be walked on in heaven.

If heaven is our forever home, and we have a forever promise that we are saved thoroughly, there's nothing too great Jesus could ask of us now. He left heaven's throne to be born in a manger, live humbly in turbulent times, die upon a cross He did not deserve, and rise victoriously for people hiding in fear. If Jesus gave us all that, we will never outgive Him. He sacrificed more than we ever could. Since He opened His arms on the cross for us, we should open our hands to Him.

Count Me In for Countercultural Contentment

You may hesitate at this step in your discipleship because of fear. You might wonder what you'll lose if you choose countercultural contentment. But have you ever thought of what you might gain? Instead of thinking about missed chances in this life, consider how your willingness to sacrifice your wants might change what others experience for eternity.

Your life can impact countless others. Let God use you by opening your hands and sharing what He has placed in them. Imagine a homeless man needing something to eat. Your dad gives you some food and supplies and encourages you to give them to the man. When you meet the man's need, you can't take credit for it; you only transferred what your father gave you.

The path toward countercultural contentment starts with evaluating all the wonderful things your heavenly Father has placed in your hands. Once you can do that, a natural progression takes place. You receive from God, and you give on behalf of God. Here are some ways to nurture countercultural contentment in your discipleship journey:

1. **REFLECT.** Developing a countercultural contentment begins with reflecting on the unique ways God has already blessed you. Look at your life and write down the possessions you've received, the constants you've taken for granted, and the blessings you've enjoyed. This process will help you take your eyes off things you've envied and focus on those things you've enjoyed.

2. **RECOGNIZE.** Go through the list you wrote and thank God through prayer for His numerous gifts. Since God is the giver of every good thing (James 1:17), let your prayers be specific. Tell God how He has cared for your needs throughout every stage of your life. The process may also lead you to thank God for those people who have provided for your needs. Take that thankfulness a step further by thanking those people for their gifts and sacrifices. It's an excellent way to follow Jesus.

3. **RELINQUISH.** Reflecting on and recognizing all God has given you should encourage you to relinquish your rights to them. A disciple of Jesus should be marked by His radical generosity. Look for ways to give to your church, to sacrifice for a missionary, or to donate to someone in need. Give now while you're young. No matter how much you have now, it will create a habit of giving when you might have more later in life. God loves to use unlikely candidates who surrender what they have so that He can do the impossible with it. Jesus once used a young boy's lunch to impact thousands of lives (John 6:9), and He will make a difference in countless more when you trust Him with what you have.

Don't let your lack of possessions discourage you or your extravagant wealth encourage you toward stinginess. Think about all God has given you and be willing to offer it to others. Can we count you in for countercultural contentment?

Insights

1. What do you wish you had right now that you don't?

   _____

   _____

   _____

   _____

   _____

2. Would you label the items you listed above as things you need or things you want?

   _____

   _____

   _____

   _____

   _____

3. What are three specific blessings God has given you?

   _____

   _____

   _____

   _____

   _____

4. How can you become more generous with what you have?

_____

_____

_____

_____

_____

5. How could you serve someone less fortunate than you?

_____

_____

_____

_____

_____

Reading Plan and Observations

Read Luke 16-18. As you read, write down what you notice about Jesus and contentment.

_____

_____

_____

_____

_____

_____

_____

_____

_____

_____

_____

_____

_____

_____

_____

_____

_____

_____

_____

_____

Discussion

If you meet with a group, study Luke 18:18–30. Discuss how Jesus points us to discipleship through countercultural contentment. Use the space below to write about something you learn.

_____

_____

_____

_____

_____

_____

_____

_____

_____

_____

_____

_____

_____

_____

_____

_____

_____

$$\sim\!\!\sim 8 \sim\!\!\sim$$

OBVIOUS OBEDIENCE

You can't follow Jesus the way He commands
if no one is aware of your commitment.

DISCIPLESHIP IS MORE THAN A checkbox of beliefs to agree with or a set of emotions to feel. Discipleship happens when the conceptual becomes practical, once the ideas become a way of life.

In the Great Commission, Jesus urged His listeners to make disciples by "teaching them to observe everything" He had commanded (Matthew 28:20). Jesus never said to teach others to believe, memorize, or repeat what He said. His goal was for them to *observe*. That word implies that information must move to application. Jesus's teachings can only be appreciated when they are applied and put into action.

The places Jesus leads us to go and how He calls us to move should be undeniable in a world that goes against His directions. If we show Him unwavering allegiance, our commitment will be impossible to hide. People will notice your change of direction. They'll notice the difference in your speech—in the words you say and the ones you don't. They'll see how you treat others, regardless of how they treat you. They'll realize you don't go along with the crowd. Obedience to Jesus rarely goes unnoticed, because you will look more like Jesus than the people and patterns of this world.

Consistently Inconsistent

Jake loved technology, so when he started going to the weekly worship gathering for students his age, he decided to serve on the media team. His skills were a great asset to the ministry. He never complained about prepping the slides ahead of time. He even brought his laptop to connect to the projector because his was a better quality than what the team had been using.

One night, the band sounded strong, the visuals looked professional, and the service was headed in a great direction. That is, until Jake changed a setting on his computer, and, during announcements, his screensaver accidentally projected onto the screen. He noticed due to people's loud gasps as they watched sensual photos of celebrities rotate on the screen. No one could reroute the awkwardness filling the room when what Jake thought to be in secret became exposed.

Can you imagine how tense that moment must have been? What if it would have been you? What if a leader took your tech, connected it, and projected your hidden world for everyone to see? If that scenario makes you cringe, it's time to make a change. That change doesn't involve leaving your computer at home—although it could. It's more about being obedient to God while using technology.

Jesus said that whatever is done in the darkness will be brought to the light (Luke 8:17). Even when we think our sin is hidden, it's never beyond God's sight. If our sin continues, it takes root and grows to the point everyone can see it.

If you've ever tried to fight temptation, you know it's a frustrating battle. You want to be obedient, but you are continually reminded of what you seem unable to do. It's disappointing when the only consistent thing is your inconsistency. Even when we have a span of eager obedience, it's challenged with the lure of doing our own thing. There's no escaping the struggle with sin, but we must keep up the fight no matter how frustrating it is. Thankfully, the Bible gives us examples and encouragement.

Jesus and Obedience

At the beginning of Luke, Jesus showed what obedience looks like. When Satan tempted Jesus with every possible temptation (Luke 4:13), Jesus remained obedient to God's Word. No one was observing Jesus's decisions, yet He revealed His reasoning in each response for our benefit.

None of us can obey God like Jesus did. We are not perfect. We make sinful decisions, and we are only saved by the gospel. But after our salvation, we still have clear directions for our path in this life. As Jesus discipled those around Him, He constantly encouraged them to obey whatever God asked.

Taking Responsibility

The Bible story about the tax collector Zacchaeus is a memorable one. This short man climbed a tree to glimpse Jesus walking by (Luke 19:4). Although it's commendable that Zacchaeus wanted to see Jesus, it's remarkable that Jesus chose to see Zacchaeus. Jesus even wanted to visit Zacchaeus in his home. This man in a tree, who felt less than others and had enraged many, had Jesus's full attention.

Zacchaeus was overwhelmed! As a chief tax collector, he had wronged many people by taking their money. He was surprised Jesus showed interest. When Jesus gave him unprovoked grace, Zacchaeus responded, "Look, I'll give half of my possessions to the poor, Lord. And if I have extorted anything from anyone, I'll pay back four times as much" (Luke 19:8).

Jesus's grace led to Zacchaeus's generosity. Jesus cared for the man first, and it was this care that led Zacchaeus to change. The tax collector made right what he had done wrong and committed to doing right in the future.

If you have received the gospel, it can cause you to come out of hiding and do the right thing too. Jesus didn't demand our obedience before loving us; His love makes us eager to obey. We should live with a growing desire to do the right thing and to make right anything we've done wrong. Let God's grace motivate you to obedience. His way is better.

Cleansing Impurity

As Jesus neared the time of His death, He traveled to Jerusalem, the capital city. While many rejoiced to see Him, many didn't, especially the greedy crooks at the temple who were swindling the people (Luke 19:45).

Jesus didn't bring these crooks near—He threw them out of the temple. He removed barriers so the people could worship God when they came to His house. The temple was meant for prayer, but the crooks had made it about how they could make a buck (Luke 19:46).

The apostle Paul once referenced a temple, but it wasn't in Jerusalem. It's you! "Don't you know that your body is a temple of the Holy Spirit who is in you, whom you have from God? You are not your own, for you were bought at a price. So glorify God with your body" (1 Corinthians 6:19–20). We are the place where God's Spirit resides. Just as Jesus got rid of the crooks in the temple, so we are to cleanse anything unholy from the temple of our bodies.

Faking Righteousness

As Jesus continued to confront unholiness, more people opposed Him. Even groups who didn't like each other conspired to shut Jesus up. His examples and teaching challenged their practices, and they wanted to eliminate Him.

How desperate did they get? "They watched closely and sent spies who pretended to be righteous, so that they could catch him in what he said, to hand him over to the governor's rule and authority" (Luke 20:20). The Bible says Jesus's opponents were only pretending to be righteous. They asked Jesus what seemed like sincere religious questions, but He saw through their crafty attempts to catch Him in His words. They didn't want to know the truth or to do what He said.

We can be guilty of faking righteousness too. Most of us are on our best behavior in the pews at church or during youth group. We know how to talk the talk and walk the walk, but our true nature reveals itself when we are in different environments. Are you actively desiring to live the right way, or are you trying to manipulate a situation to get away with what you want to do? Don't pretend to be righteous—pursue righteousness by obeying Jesus's commands.

Acknowledging Traps

In one of Jesus's final conversations with His disciples, He warned them about the trap of sin. He knew difficult times were coming for them, and He understood temptation's power. Jesus warned the disciples to be on guard. From who? From what? He didn't tell them to worry about the Jewish leaders, the Roman government, or even the devil. Jesus warned them about a more ominous threat—themselves. "Be on your guard, so that your minds are not dulled from carousing, drunkenness, and worries of life, or that day will come on you unexpectedly like a trap" (Luke 21:34–35).

The same holds true today. Sinful habits are dangerous traps. We draw near sin, thinking we can walk away whenever we desire. But the closer we get, the less we can discern where we are versus where God has called us to be. We tell ourselves we can stop whenever we want, yet we don't. The party life tempts us to do sinful things we regret for a long time. Drugs decrease our ability to make wise decisions. We say we will get out of that tempting relationship if it worsens, but our emotions blind us to reality. We can be so dulled by our sinful choices that we can't even tell we're caught in the trap.

What is the most dangerous trap for you? Your struggle with sin won't be the same as everyone else's. Everyone is tempted, but certain temptations are more successful on some of us than others.

Do you ever feel stuck in the same type of sin? You may want to stop, but you find yourself in the middle of it, deeper than before. The apostle Paul thought the same thing. "For I do not do the good that I want to do, but I practice the evil that I do not want to do" (Romans 7:19). If you desire a change but can't get the willpower to do it, there's hope for you. You don't have to stay defeated, entangled in the same sin.

Changing Up

You won't fall into obedience by accident. You must change your habits to see hopeful transformation. Discipleship is learning the way of Jesus, believing it to be better than any other path in the world, and learning to walk like Him in every situation.

Your first focus needs to be desiring obedience. You must develop the perspective that Jesus's way is better than your personal preferences. If you feel like you are being forced to do something, you will lack motivation. But obedience to Jesus is not what you *have* to do; it is what you *get* to do.

When the apostle Paul mentored his young disciple Timothy, he encouraged him to love and obey God by "flee[ing] from youthful passions, and pursue righteousness, faith, love, and peace, along with those who call on the Lord from a pure heart" (2 Timothy 2:22).

What are youthful passions? They are the urges you feel more acutely as a young person. Temptations don't end once you move out of teenage status, but some seem very persistent during these years. Lust, for instance, is a desire for anything you don't need. It is a hunger for something that shouldn't be on the table. Paul told Timothy to flee that urge, among others.

When Paul said to flee youthful passions, he didn't mean Timothy should see how close he could get to those things without touching them. Flee meant run for your life! The motivation to run comes from two places. First, the belief that God's commands are meant to increase your joy, and second, that the urge, whatever it is, must be dangerous. When you believe those things, it is easier to run from the youthful passions God says are out to get you. Obeying God's commands doesn't keep you from the fun parts of life; it allows you to enjoy the excellent things more.

When you were young, you might have been frustrated when your parents wouldn't let you play on the road. You might have thought they were against having fun, but were they? No. They were trying to keep you safe so that you could play much longer.

Our heavenly Father is the same. When He says not to do something, He says it for our good. Once we understand His intention, we are much more prone to run away from sin and toward righteousness.

Paul's command to Timothy has two instructions that can be obeyed at the same time: flee from danger and run to delight. It's not two different directions. They're the same. We need to see what we want to avoid while pursuing the better things we want to obtain. You can't just tell yourself to avoid sin; you must encourage yourself by remembering you are seeking something better. Saying "no" to something now is saying "yes" to something later. We must replace bad habits with good ones, or our minds, wills, and hands will drift back toward danger.

So flee from the temptation tripping you up, and run toward Jesus. But don't forget the last words of 2 Timothy 2:22: "along with those who call on the Lord from a pure heart." You can't run by yourself. When you are trying to get somewhere, it's best to run alongside people who are going in the same direction. Run from sin, run toward righteousness, and run with those who are heading in the same direction.

Count Me In for Obvious Obedience

Jesus gathered His disciples around a table for one last teaching the night before He was crucified. He told them, "If you love me, you will keep my commands" (John 14:15). We often imagine people who love Jesus as those with passionate expressions of worship or committed times of prayer. That's often true, but Jesus said that *obedience* was the true proof that someone genuinely loved Him.

The order is critical. If you love Jesus first, then you will desire to obey Him. You won't see His commands as chores. You will move Jesus's way from requirement to privilege. Your love for Jesus is proven by how you obey Him on all days, in all ways.

Such dedication to Jesus means you accept the things He encourages and deny the things He forbids. You begin to see the brilliance of His commands. It also means honestly evaluating your life and making needed changes. How do you examine your life to see where you need to change?

1. **ACKNOWLEDGE.** This step shouldn't take long, but it is essential. Evaluate your most frustrating temptations. What areas of sin do you fall into the most? You know what you struggle with the most when no one else is around, and you know what you've repeatedly done in front of others. Acknowledge those sin areas.

2. **ADMIT.** God is not surprised by your sins, so go ahead and admit them to Him. In confession, we realize it is safe to be honest with the One who already knows everything. To act as if we have no sin is to add lying to our record (1 John 1:8). When we confess our sins, God doesn't run away. He forgives us (1 John 1:9). In addition

to admitting our sins to God, we should share them with someone else. We discover a spiritual type of healing when we confess our sins to one another (James 5:16).

3. **ASK.** After we have acknowledged and admitted our sin to ourselves, God, and another person, we should ask for help. Did you know God can help you in temptation? Jesus faced temptation and knows how to help (Hebrews 2:18). Whenever we are tempted, God provides a way of escape (1 Corinthians 10:13). God also helps by surrounding us with disciples who can bring us back to God when we sin. Agree together on a plan to fight against sin and work toward obedience. Allow them to ask you difficult questions, and promise to be honest with them. Such help can stop a multitude of sins from continuing (James 5:20).

We have a Savior who invites us to tell Him about our shortcomings, and He provides us with people who can give us the support we need. Don't settle for an obedience out of duty. Obey God because you love God. Follow Jesus unashamedly in every area of your life. Can we count you in for obvious obedience?

Insights

1. Why is it easier to behave when people are watching?

   _____

   _____

   _____

   _____

   _____

2. What do you prove about your discipleship when you choose to obey when only God sees it?

   _____

   _____

   _____

   _____

   _____

3. What sorts of temptations are most likely to keep you from following Jesus?

   _____

   _____

   _____

   _____

   _____

4. Who can you talk with about your struggles with sin?

_____

_____

_____

_____

_____

5. What should your strategy be for fighting temptation?

_____

_____

_____

_____

_____

Reading Plan and Observations

Read Luke 19-21. Write down what you notice about Jesus and obedience.

_____

_____

_____

_____

_____

_____

_____

_____

_____

_____

_____

_____

_____

_____

_____

_____

_____

_____

Discussion

If you meet with a group, study Luke 19:1–10. Discuss how Jesus points us to discipleship through obvious obedience. Use the space below to write about something you learn.

_____

_____

_____

_____

_____

_____

_____

_____

_____

_____

_____

_____

_____

_____

_____

_____

_____

_____

~~~ 9 ~~~

WILLING WITNESS

When you truly comprehend what Jesus has done
for you, you are eager to tell others about it.

NOTHING CAN STRIKE FEAR INTO the heart of a disciple quite like the expectation to share Christ with another person. It's not a youth thing either. All ages can feel afraid when explaining the gospel to another person.

Why? We eagerly and easily share a status update about a vacation, post about our favorite team, or tell another person about the great meal we had. But we freeze when it comes to sharing our faith. For some reason, we talk easily about trivial matters and uncomfortably about eternal truths.

All the priorities of discipleship described in this book are critical for your success, but this trait distinguishes you quicker than any other. If we truly comprehend all Jesus has done for us, then we should be eager to be a willing witness and tell others about what we've seen Jesus do in our lives.

If Christianity were only about how good we are, that would be a sad religion to share. Talk about disappointing! But we're not telling people about how well we have done; we are celebrating and sharing how good Christ is. And that's why it shouldn't be challenging to share Him with others.

Redefining Christians

If you decide to take the risk and talk to people about your faith, you might begin with a simple question: "Are you a Christian?" Have you ever thought about what that question means?

After Jesus's death and resurrection, His disciples began to spread the news everywhere. The movement was so new that the followers were not yet united under a name. "The disciples were first called Christians at Antioch" (Acts 11:26). Notice that the disciples didn't call themselves Christians, but people in this city gave them that name.

The term literally meant "little Christs," and it wasn't necessarily meant as an encouragement. Many historians believe the term was used in a derogatory manner to indicate the disciples were following a dead leader and were probably going to end up on death row just like He did.

Although "Christian" is only used three times in the New Testament (Acts 11:26; 26:28; 1 Peter 4:16), "disciple" is used more than 260 times. That should tell us there is no distinction between a Christian and a disciple. To follow Jesus means to do things the way He does and to invest in others. If you are a disciple, you are growing and helping others grow as well.

The Bible uses another phrase to describe Jesus-followers: "The Way" (Acts 9:2; 19:9, 23; 22:4; 24:14, 22). Jesus's disciples were not referred to as a building to visit, an event to attend, or a belief system to hold but a way to go. Why would they call themselves that? Because they knew you can't follow Jesus unless you are going somewhere. To be a disciple means you are a disciple-maker. More than a belief to have, it is a way to take. As you follow Jesus on His path, you bring others with you. We do not have a small elite group of disciples among a great multitude of Christians. To belong to Jesus means to be on the path of discipleship.

Jesus and the Mission

Jesus's final days reveal the lowest of lows and the highest of highs. Jesus died on the cross, and His disciples were clueless about what to do next. As hopelessness set in, they were amazed to discover Jesus had defeated death. Within the span of a few days, the greatest tragedy in the world turned into the most significant miracle in history.

You might think Jesus would want to keep His disciples together to protect them, but He gathered them in to send them out. On Resurrection Day and after, Jesus told His followers to go, spread the news.

Anticipating Failure

Hours before Jesus's death, He warned His disciples about the coming opposition. He wasn't concerned about His safety or outcome; He was concerned about theirs. He said Satan was targeting them, which must have been frightening to hear. Jesus told Peter, "But I have prayed for you that your faith may not fail. And you, when you have turned back, strengthen your brothers" (Luke 22:32).

You might wonder if Peter had difficulty believing he would fail. Jesus knew the failure was coming and didn't sugarcoat the situation for Peter. In Jesus's loneliest hour, Peter was nowhere to be found. He denied knowing Jesus. It wasn't a question of if Peter would fail, but of what he would do when he did.

It might not sound encouraging to anticipate failure as we follow Jesus, but we will not always get it right. Just like Peter, we will make unthinkable mistakes. If we had to prove our perfect ability, we would be in trouble, but that's not what the gospel teaches. We are loved even though we mess up. We have a Savior who prays we will rise every time we fail (Hebrews 7:25).

Embracing Grace

Peter denied Jesus, Judas betrayed Him, and the remaining disciples scattered, unsure of what to do. Jesus's enemies conspired and crucified Him next to two criminals. While the criminals were hung for sins they had committed, Jesus hung on the cross for ours. He suffered in our place.

As Jesus drew near His death, the two criminals argued about what Jesus ought to do. One criminal yelled at Jesus, demanding to be released (Luke 23:39). The other had a different perspective. He knew he deserved to die, and he believed Jesus had done nothing wrong. This criminal admitted his sinfulness, proclaimed Jesus's righteousness, and then initiated a faith-filled request. "Jesus, remember me when you come into your kingdom" (Luke 23:42). Jesus reassured him his request would become a reality that very day (Luke 23:43).

Is it difficult to believe the thief made it to heaven? If you doubt he could have made it, then there's no chance for any of us. This man, who had broken laws and endangered people, received an acceptance into heaven, and he was never able to seek baptism, join a church, give an offering, or go on a mission trip. Yet Jesus emphatically confirmed his eternal destination. Had the man been able to get off his cross, he would have followed Jesus for the sake of the mission. While he was never afforded that opportunity, we are. This pivotal moment on the cross reminds us that no one is too far gone. No one's sin can outdo God's grace. If that criminal could receive salvation, so can anyone with whom you share the gospel. You can marvel at the grace you have experienced and embrace the message of the gospel as the hope for anyone you encounter.

Sharing Amazement

The end of the Gospel of Luke records Jesus's remarkable resurrection. The somber women and the fearful disciples never saw it coming, even though Jesus had told them numerous times. When some of these women showed up Sunday morning to perform burial procedures, they were ready for the difficult task of caring for their deceased teacher's body. What they found was an empty tomb with angels present but Jesus absent.

"Why are you looking for the living among the dead?" the angels asked (Luke 24:5). Their message confused the women. They couldn't believe it, but they couldn't stay there either. What did they do? They went and told people the tomb was empty (Luke 24:9). Some believed, and others didn't, but that didn't stop the women from telling all who would listen. Jesus was alive, and they had to share their amazement with others.

We should follow their example. Too often, we complicate sharing the gospel with others, wasting a tremendous amount of time worrying about methods. The heart of evangelism is telling another person how you know the risen Christ.

Don't stay at the tomb; Jesus isn't there! Tell others what you have experienced. Share your gratitude for Jesus's crucifixion and your amazement at His resurrection.

Starting Here

In the last few paragraphs of Luke, Jesus gathered His disciples together to share some important instructions. These instructions are the Great Commission, which appears in each Gospel (Matthew, Mark, Luke, and John). In Luke, Jesus told His disciples that "repentance for forgiveness of sins will be proclaimed in his name to all the nations, beginning at Jerusalem. You are witnesses of these things" (Luke 24:47–48).

The gospel of Jesus is incredible. The whole world needs to hear it! You might be overwhelmed by that thought. It might be a challenge to imagine taking the gospel to the other side of the world when you are just trying to make it to high school graduation. Read Jesus's words again. The nations do need to hear the gospel. But the disciples needed to start where they were, and so do you.

The disciples were in Jerusalem, and you are in your hometown. You don't have to wonder if there are people who don't know Jesus near you. They are here, there, and everywhere. We pray you get the opportunity to share Jesus with people on the other side of the world, but you first need to give that message to someone on the other side of your classroom. The more comfortable you get with sharing Jesus where you live, the easier it will be to share that message when you go far away.

Whenever you feel inadequate to obey Jesus's instructions, remember He hasn't left you alone. He encouraged the disciples with the promise of the Holy Spirit, who would strengthen them all along the way. That hasn't changed. No matter where we are, the Holy Spirit is there with us. As we go, He goes. The Holy Spirit empowers us to be willing witnesses.

We have observed what Jesus has done through His life and in our lives, and we should be ready to tell others about it.

Speaking Up

If you want to take discipleship seriously, you've got to take the next step. Give away what you've received. Showing up in discipleship means being intentional in developing another person. Telling all nations about Jesus might be a challenging request at this point in your life. Putting the entire world's evangelization efforts on your shoulders might be too much to consider if you hope to make it through this school year in one piece.

The thing is, while reaching the whole world for Christ is not on your shoulders, God does expect you to reach someone. The worldwide church has received the Great Commission, and together, we will eventually minister to all nations.

Where do you start? With one person. The church will reach the world as individual disciples reach one person at a time. The task is great, but it will be accomplished by willing witnesses who take small steps of faith. Who is the one person you need to reach? Who are you ready to teach? Out of all the people around you, who is the next person you can focus on and attempt to reach for the cause of Christ?

Evangelism introduces someone to Jesus, and discipleship teaches someone to follow Jesus after that initial step of faith. As a reminder, the goal is not to make converts (those who say they believe); we are called to make disciples (those who say they will follow). For this step in your discipleship journey, you must encourage someone in their faith development. You might disciple one of these people . . .

1. An unbeliever. You share the gospel in the hope that they will believe it and desire to follow Jesus.
2. Someone who claims to follow Christ but is just starting to learn how to do it. You can teach them some initial steps to get going.
3. A person who claims to be a Christian but shows little evidence of it. You can help them understand that discipleship is a faith that acts.
4. A fellow believer. You might get the thrill of seeing someone grow because you commit to walking alongside them.

Those four examples have one thing in common: helping one person move one step closer to Jesus. That's all discipleship is. As you evaluate where one person is spiritually, you either invite them to believe or help them take their next steps in discipleship. It can't be a cookie-cutter approach, attempting to do the same thing for every person. Everyone is in a different spot and requires specific instructions, but we all need an example a few steps ahead who will point us in the right direction.

Count Me In for Willing Witness

You are ready to be a witness to others. You have more knowledge than you think you do. You're about to finish reading through the Gospel of Luke and a book guiding you through discipleship concepts. That shows you are taking your faith seriously. You have valuable knowledge to share.

We all struggle to communicate certain biblical concepts with another person. Each disciple of Jesus still has areas of sin they struggle to overcome. But you cannot wait until you achieve mastery in your Bible trivia or perfection in your personal holiness to start training someone else. Take what you have and give it to another person.

Resolve in your mind that Jesus has saved you so amazingly that you can't help but share Him with others. You aren't bragging about yourself; you're bragging about Christ. That should be easy for any disciple to do! Here are some ways you can begin:

1. **INQUIRE.** Whether sharing the gospel with an unbeliever or discipling another believer, ask Jesus who you should reach out to. The individual may live down the hall or down the street, but people who need Jesus are all around you. Most likely, you will consider someone who is either not a believer yet or someone who is a few steps behind you in their faith. It could be a younger sibling or underclassman in the youth group. It might be a classmate who is new to faith. Pray and ask God who you need to reach.

2. **INITIATE.** Evangelism or discipleship must begin with you initiating conversations. Make these interactions as natural as you can. You are simply making yourself available to another person. Your message is not how great you are but how amazing Jesus is. You might be surprised at how thankful they are that you care about their spiritual condition. Communicate that you want to teach them what God has taught you.

3. **INVEST.** Once you begin communicating with this individual, give everything away. What you take for granted might be a game changer for your friend. You have so much to offer through all the resources you have used, the sermons you have heard, the examples you have seen, and the opportunities you have received. Share how you are enduring struggles. Tell stories of how God came through when it seemed impossible. Provide lessons you are learning from your time in the Word or from those who have taught you.

You don't have bad news to share; they call it good news for a reason. Keep that in mind as you share what you know to be true about Jesus with another person. Can we count you in as a willing witness? ·₊˙

Insights

1. What is your greatest fear when sharing about Christ with another person?

_____

_____

_____

_____

_____

2. How could you brag about Jesus to another person? What would you say?

_____

_____

_____

_____

_____

3. Who is someone you feel God is asking you to reach out to?

_____

_____

_____

_____

4. How will you initiate the first conversation?

_____

_____

_____

_____

_____

5. What do you plan to share first?

_____

_____

_____

_____

_____

Reading Plan and Observations

Read Luke 22–24. As you read, write down what you notice about Jesus and being a witness to others.

_____

_____

_____

_____

_____

_____

_____

_____

_____

_____

_____

_____

_____

_____

_____

_____

_____

_____

_____

Discussion

If you meet with a group, study Luke 24:13–35. Discuss how Jesus points us to discipleship through being a willing witness. Use the space below to write about something you learn.

CONCLUSION

CONGRATULATIONS! NOT ONLY HAVE YOU made it to the end of this book, but you have also studied the Gospel of Luke and discovered the path of discipleship by following the Master. Watching how Jesus lived His life and made disciples is an unbelievable view. His investment in disciples changed the world, and here you are, centuries later, on the other side of the world, still unpacking all His simple yet profound ways of discipleship.

You have finished this book, but that doesn't mean you have finished discipleship. This marvelous adventure will continue throughout your life. We aren't going to print out a disciple certificate as if you are done and can move on to the next thing. There is no other thing after discipleship—it is *the* thing. You have the excellent opportunity to continue growing in holiness, developing your skills, and sharing through service, evangelism, and discipleship. As you learn from Jesus through the Word of God and the people of God around you, carry those lessons and give them away to future disciples.

Here's another good thing: you can take the principles outlined in this book, the ones we gleaned from Jesus's example, and keep using them to go deeper in your discipleship.

1. **DILIGENT DEVOTIONS.** You have completed Luke, but that doesn't mean you get to put your Bible away. Decide on the next book or Bible reading plan you'll begin today.